Foreword By His Holiness

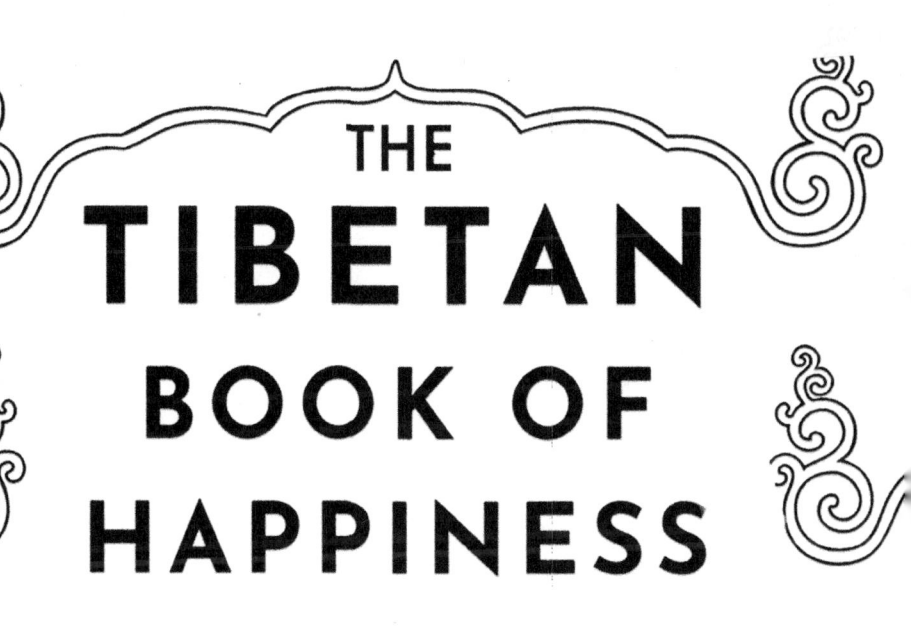

THE TIBETAN BOOK OF HAPPINESS

REVEALING THE GREATEST YET SIMPLEST SECRET

6TH GARAB TULKU LOBSANG DHONDEN

Badawa Academy Press

© 2024 by 6th Garab Tulku Lobsang Dhonden

All rights reserved. No part of this book may be reproduced in any form or by any means, electronic or mechanical, including photocopying, recording, or by any information storage and retrieval system, without permission in writing from the publisher.

Published by Badawa Academy Press

www.badawa-academy.org

Library of Congress control number: 2023918218

ISBN 9 798218 191559(paperback)

Cover Design by Asia Bizior
Interior & back cover design by Natalia Junqueira

First Edition: 2024

Printed in the United States of America

THE TIBETAN BOOK OF HAPPINESS

A New Lens:
Transforming How You See Yourself,
Others , and Life

To His Holiness the Dalai Lama, a beacon of wisdom and compassion, whose guidance inspires us all to seek inner peace and understanding.

To the resilient Tibetan people, guardians of a rich and unique cultural heritage.

May this book honor your legacy and the timeless wisdom you embody.

In loving memory of my beloved grandma and father,
whose unwavering love and compassion
have forever been the pillar of my inner strength.

Rest in peace in Kechara.

CONTENTS

Foreword by His Holiness the Dalai Lama x
Foreword by HE Zong Rinpoche xii

Preface 1
Homage 3

Happiness 9
Temporary Happiness 10
Lasting Happiness 16
Why Lasting Happiness Is Possible? 24
Mind, Our New World 32
Rigpa 39
    Sensory Mind 40
    Conceptual Mind 41
    Cognitive Mind 45
    Memory Mind 45
    Emotional Mind 46
    Feeling Mind 47
Mind Is the Mastermind of Everything 48
Law of Karma, the 'Judicial System' of the Inner World 53
Selwa — Clarity — the Greatest Secret of Mind 58
Fundamental Positivity 64
Negative Potential 74

Meditation, Path of the Inner World of Mind 79
What Is Meditation? How Does It Work? 81
    Subject 85
    Object 86
    Function 87
    Measure of Actual Meditation 89
The Actual Way to Develop Lasting Happiness 92
Foundation Path 95
    Mechanism of Worry 97
    How To Calm Worry 99
        Returning Home, the Fundamental Nature of Mind 100
        Performing a Reality Check on Problems 101
        Turning Off the Problem-Worry Link 107
    The Foundation Path Meditation 111
    Measure of Realization of the Foundation Path 114
The Vast Path 115
    How to Enhance Fundamental Positivity 115
    Finding *Selwa* (Fundamental Positivity) 116
    Actual Method to Enhance Fundamental Positivity 117
    Vast Path Guided Meditation 123
    Visual Guided Meditation on How to Enhance Your Fundamental Positivity 125
    Measure of Realization of the Vast Path 129
Profound Path 130
    The Way to Reduce Negativity 130
        How root negativity conceives its object 131
        How root negativity causes all other afflictions by conceiving the way it does 133

Identifying self-grasping in daily life 135
Examining if the conceived object can withstand a reality check ... 136
How root negativity and derivative negativities can be eradicated
    if its conceived object is proven non-existent 140

Wisdom Path Meditation Guide 143
Measure of Realization of the Wisdom Path 147

A Glimpse of Great Nirvana, the Pinnacle of Lasting
Happiness 149

Path of Accumulation 153
Path of Preparation 155
    Four Divisions of the Path of Preparation 158
Path of Seeing 160
Path of Meditation 162
Path of No-More-Training 164

Glossary 165
Acknowledgments 179
The Badawa Academy Curriculum and Its Mission 181
About the Author 184

THE DALAI LAMA

Foreword

We all want to be happy, we don't want to suffer, but both conditions relate to our mental state. Transforming our mind is the root of happiness. Today, the world is mostly focussed on external development. However, ancient Indian traditions that we have kept alive to this day emphasise the mind as the real source of happiness, so it is our minds we have to transform.

We all have seeds of compassion, loving-kindness and concern for others within us on the basis of which we can build a happy human community. In my own experience, when we were still in Tibet, we thought of the outside world and people in it as different from us, but once we became refugees, we became aware of the oneness of humanity and understood that all human beings are basically the same.

I believe that the purpose of life is to lead a happy life. However, real happiness is not about having money or power, it's about achieving inner peace. If we have peace of mind, we will be happy day and night. Happiness is related to our emotions. And we all have the potential to experience positive as well as negative emotions. It is therefore important to cultivate warm heartedness and compassion with a concern for the well-being of others.

As Garab Tulku discusses in "The Tibetan Book of Happiness" we can learn how to cultivate peace of mind. We can then employ our intelligence to extend our compassion on an individual, family, community and global level. Through training and familiarity we can learn to appreciate the oneness of the eight billion human beings alive today and help to lead a meaningful life.

With my prayers and good wishes,

18 April 2024

Foreword

I am honored to have been asked by Garab Tulku Lobsang Dhonden to write the foreword for The Tibetan Book of Happiness, a book which draws together Buddhist philosophy and Rinpoche's personal experiences to create a practical, accessible and contemporary path to realizing the potential for lasting happiness that resides within each human being, whether a practicing Buddhist or not.

As a young monk when I was beginning basic studies on logic at Gaden Shartse Monastic University, I admired the exceptional intellect Garab Tulku demonstrated during the Prajnaparamita and Madhyamika debates, part of his Geshe Degree studies. Since then, I have followed Rinpoche's progress and have been impressed by how his simple approach to teachings, lectures, and healing sessions has brought happiness to audiences in many countries around the world.

As His Holiness the Dalai Lama says, we are all the same human beings. We are born the same way, we die the same way, and we all want to lead happy lives. I am certain that The Tibetan Book of Happiness will help many to connect more meaningfully with their own inner happiness in the years to come.

28-6-2023

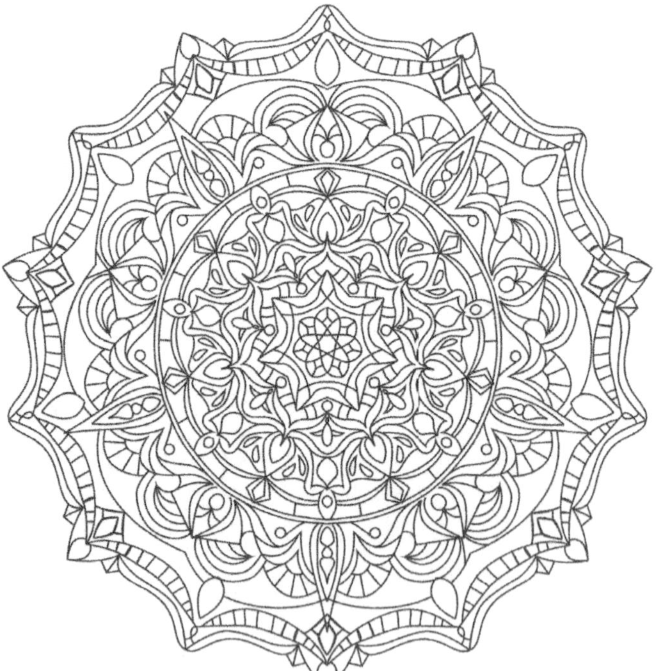

Preface

Books on Buddhist subjects are plentiful today, you can simply google a topic from the Buddhist Canon and have some information. My intention in writing this book, however, is not to simply restate the Buddhist philosophy that I have studied for the past thirty years. Many of my friends at the monastery and elsewhere suggested that I write the book in Tibetan and have it translated. That is not what I want. I aim for it to appeal to a universal audience, grounded in principles that resonate across cultures, countries, and communities. It is also much influenced by my experiences teaching in English to international audiences.

I had accumulated a great deal of knowledge of Buddhism when my grandmother's death affected me so powerfully as I will describe below. I was shocked to find my equilibrium so disturbed, and it inspired me to go back to the scriptures to see how I could really apply them for myself. In doing so I developed the meditative techniques described in this book. They helped me to overcome some very difficult experiences. I have brought them out of the technical language of the scriptures, however, and describe them in simple English as best I can. I apologize for any mistakes or deviations from standard writing style that may be present in the book. As per my agreement with my editor, we have opted for a light editing approach in order to preserve the conversational tone and informal essence of my writing. I have made every effort to convey the intended meaning accurately throughout the book. Please accept my apologies in advance for any errors that may have occurred.

I suggest thinking of it like a cookbook for happiness. In going back to the scriptures, I found the ingredients for the recipes presented here. But you are the one who has to do the cooking! Feel free to season them with your own herbs and spices as you make them your own!

This book is also an exploration of our shared human nature, our mind and its deepest treasury of secrets. To unravel the ultimate meaning of life, Buddha tried to tackle the two most profound questions of all: 'Is mind fundamentally positive?' and 'Can negativity be permanently removed?' You can think of this book as a do-it-yourself manual to explore these questions for yourself. Those who feel particularly drawn to these questions, who would like to enroll in a program of more rigorous training, I invite to inquire about the course I will be offering at my soon-to-be-founded Buddhist Academy. Some detail on what this will include can be found at the end of this book.

Today, the world is still ravaged by damage caused by the pandemic and war. The death toll rises and people face tremendous difficulties. More than ever we need ways to relieve worry and anxiety and to experience more happiness. The methods I describe herein have definitely helped me when my emotional equilibrium was disturbed, which makes me optimistic that they may be of benefit to you as well.

6th Garab Tulku Lobsang Dhonden
Huntington Beach, California
July 14, 2024

Namo Guru Manjugoshaya

Ceaselessly roaring thunder of profound *shunyata*
from monsoon clouds in sky of interdependence,
pouring down timely rain to cool tormenting heat
    of self-grasping,
to the moving clouds of compassion of Buddha,
    the peerless teacher, I pay homage.

    (-Khedrubje)

It was around six in the morning when my phone rang. My father was on the line. "Mo-la (grandma) is not waking up," he said in a faint voice. Confused, I asked him what he meant. He told me to rush home immediately. I kick-started my motorbike and raced home. When I reached home, I walked straight into my grandmother's bedroom and saw her lying on her side, breathing hoarsely. Her eyes were slightly open, but I assumed she couldn't see. I sat beside her and talked to her. There was no response. "Mo-la" I cried at the top of my lungs. This time she appeared to have heard me. She tried very hard to look at me, garnering every bit of energy she still had left. I uttered "Om Mani Padme Hung," the sacred mantra of Chenrezig, Buddha of compassion, loudly into her ear. To our surprise, she repeated the mantra, though with slurred pronunciation. I remember that moment vividly. It was the saddest day of my life as I knew she was dying. She was lying in the sleeping-lion-posture like our historical Buddha did when he passed into Parinirvana. My grandmother died later that evening. The fact that she was lying in that posture has been of some solace to me and my parents because we believe that this posture alone protects one from taking rebirth in a suffering realm of existence.

The day before had been a grand opening of the newly built temple of *Phukhang Khangtsen,* one of the 11 houses within *Gaden Shartse* Monastery. After the inauguration ceremony held in the morning, I went straight to pay a visit to my grandma to share the offerings I had received, consisting of Tibetan ritual cakes and fruits. I spent almost the whole day conversing with her, touching on different aspects of life. At sunset, as I was preparing to leave for the monastery, she asked "Why don't you stay tonight here with me?" I replied that I had to go back to the monastery because the next morning a highly revered reincarnate lama was leaving for Europe and I had to see him off. The next morning, instead of seeing off the lama, I had to rush back home and say my final goodbye to her.

The death of my grandma was shocking to me. She had been the pillar of our family, and hers was the first death I had experienced in our family. She had been more of a mother than a grandmother to me, as a good portion of my childhood was spent with her in a mountainous region of Bhutan while my parents were away, working in the Bhutanese town of Paro. The fact that I hadn't stayed that night, as she had asked, made my grief at losing her even harder to bear. After her funeral, I would often lie in bed during the day with all the curtains closed, then listen to her voice which I had recorded during the many beautiful times we had in the past. On one of the tapes, she described how she performed her customary dedication prayer before going to bed. Her dedications encompassed the well-being of her children and grandchildren, the long life of His Holiness the Dalai Lama, peace on earth without famine, pandemics, and natural disasters. She concluded her prayer by dedicating all merit for the welfare of all mother sentient beings. Her majestic voice, brimming with sincerity and honesty, provided solace to my troubled mind. I frequently sought refuge in the confines of my dark room, finding solace in listening to those cherished tapes.

Several friends of mine had noticed changes in my behavior and temperament. I became increasingly susceptible to mental suffering, experiencing worry, fear, anxiety, and depression more easily and intensely. Additionally, I developed a persistent headache that lingered despite my attempts to alleviate it with Anacin, a commonly used medication available at our monastery shop.

From that moment onward I made a firm resolve to delve deeper into understanding the alleviation of mental suffering. I revisited all the monastic treatises I had previously studied and carefully scrutinized them, employing reasoning and internalization to extract essential instructions. This introspective process proved to be highly beneficial.

Before this I had unconsciously held a dismissive attitude toward students from western developed nations who sought guidance from our master to address their numerous problems and mental anguish. However, my perspective shifted drastically after that pivotal moment. I found myself empathizing with their struggles and empathetic towards anyone who experienced suffering, especially of the mental kind. My empathy became even stronger for those who may not fully understand what is happening to them. I now understood the complexity of these issues.

Prior to this transformative experience, I had often assumed the role of an unofficial therapist among my friends, approaching their difficulties with simplistic questions such as, "Why are you depressed?" or offering solutions like, "Just be happy!" or "Why can't you think positively?" or "Leave your mind alone!" I naively believed that mental happiness was easily attainable and solely a matter of shifting one's mindset. However, my own personal journey contradicted this simplistic view. Thus, embarking on my pursuit of happiness and relief from suffering, I gained a profound appreciation for the intricacies involved.

I am delighted to share my discoveries about something fundamental and invaluable to all living beings: happiness. The pursuit of happiness and the alleviation of suffering have been driving forces in the cycle of life since the dawn of human evolution and, from a Buddhist perspective, since beginningless time. This is precisely why I am writing this book—to impart my thoughts on how to attain happiness, which brings me immense joy in itself. The paths to happiness that I will outline in this book draw inspiration from the wisdom of Buddha and Je Tsongkhapa, the fourteenth-century Tibetan scholar who established the Geluk school of Tibetan Buddhism. I will also incorporate insights from my own life experiences.

The method I am about to reveal for experiencing happiness delves into the very core of our existence as living beings. It unveils our most precious possession, our deepest secret, and unlocks our infinite potential. Yet, it is simple, natural, and unassuming. Therefore, this book is dedicated to all human beings—regardless of race, ethnicity, religion, or belief—whether they identify as Christians, Buddhists, Muslims, Jews, Hindus, atheists, or any other category. It is my heartfelt aspiration that people of all religions become the best versions of themselves, that atheists find greater happiness, and that Buddhists pursue Great Nirvana with renewed dedication.

It is undeniable that all living beings, including you and I, strive throughout our lives is to experience happiness and to avoid suffering. Human beings, due to our intelligence, have more resources for this than other lifeforms. We have discovered religions, arts, sciences, systems of law and justice; we have invented everything possible to generate, sustain, and enhance happiness. Beggars beg, sweepers sweep, workers work, bankers bank, teachers teach, businessmen sell, mothers love, politicians govern, spiritualists pray, monks meditate – all for happiness. If you doubt this, ask yourself, and you will find the answer within. Even a person who claims to have shunned happiness does so for the sake of happiness!

If there is one common aspiration that unites all beings—regardless of their religious or non-religious affiliations, even extending to animals and insects—it is the universal pursuit of happiness. What distinguishes us are the methods we employ in our quest for happiness. The purpose of this book is to introduce avenues to happiness that are fundamental, natural, simple, and universally applicable, while also being verifiable through personal experience and deepening of wisdom.

Happiness differs from person to person in terms of its causes and what we perceive it to be. A cause of happiness for one can even be a cause of suffering for others. For me, being on my own with a laptop, writing this book while relaxing with a cup of coffee and a croissant, watching people pass by from every walk of life, is a source of happiness. This may not be true for others, particularly those who dislike caffeine and want to avoid calories!

Although happiness may vary in terms of intensity and causes, its nature is the same for all in that it is subjective and cannot be duplicated. Real happiness cannot be faked, forced, or obtained by just thinking of it. Happiness has to be genuine and natural. It occurs on the level of emotion and feelings so it is not just a thought process. If it was, acquiring happiness might be quite easy!

Happiness cannot be adequately expressed in words. It must be felt inside and experienced like no other phenomenon. It is therefore easiest to understand from a first-person perspective. We can fully appreciate happiness by feeling it and, based on this, infer what happiness is for others. We cannot feel our mother's happiness exactly the same way she does, but we can understand it and infer how it feels based on our own experience of happiness. Because of this, we feel happy when our mother is happy, even though the happiness we feel is not the same happiness that our mother feels, and vice-versa.

HAPPINESS

So, what is happiness, really? The fact that all living beings live in pursuit of happiness clearly shows that we, in some way, know what happiness is. We all have had firsthand experiences of happiness; we wouldn't be pursuing something we know nothing about! However, in order to know happiness in its entirety, we must know our own mind. Happiness is a facet of our mind and therefore it is subjective. It is a feeling that must be enjoyed, felt and experienced. Science has created many beautiful things that stimulate happiness, but not happiness itself. The nature of happiness, in its very subjective aspect, is unique to first person experience. It would be as impossible to explain as the sweetness of honey! There are many attributes of happiness, however, that can be easily understood by anyone. Based on those attributes, and for ease of understanding, I categorize and simplify happiness as twofold: temporary happiness and lasting happiness.

TEMPORARY HAPPINESS

Temporary happiness is momentary and not sustainable. Depending on its various attributes, temporary happiness includes dependent happiness, materially-creatable-happiness, conditional happiness, superficial happiness, suffering of change and so on.

Most of the happiness we experience in our lives is temporary. This can be further divided into two categories: temporary physical happiness and temporary mental happiness. These two comprise the typical happiness we enjoy during our life. Temporary physical happiness is a pleasant sensation that arises from physical stimuli. Temporary mental happiness is a psychological state that is associated with physical happiness; it also very much depends upon physical stimulus. Hence, it is called 'dependent happiness.' When we listen to music we like, it gives a pleasant sensation to our auditory consciousness, which in turn gives rise to mental happiness. Both these happinesses are called 'dependent' because they are dependent upon physical happiness and material objects. These two are also known as

TEMPORARY HAPPINESS

materially-creatable-happiness due to the fact that they can be created by material things. In the winter, when a chilly morning gives way to beautiful sunlight that provides warmth, you experience a physical happiness. As soon as this happens, you feel content and pleased; this is dependent mental happiness. As you can see, the physical happiness arises in dependence upon warm sunlight, and temporary mental happiness arises as a result of having experienced that physical happiness. These two types of happiness are most of the happiness with which we are familiar. We have been chasing this happiness even though, deep inside, we have always wished for something lasting, and genuine.

What is wrong with this kind of happiness? If nothing was wrong with it this world would have become a paradise by now, because the world is full of temporary happiness! This kind of happiness, however, has many drawbacks – the biggest one being that it is temporary and impossible to sustain for a long period of time. Eventually, it not only degenerates from happiness, it turns into its opposite, suffering. Furthermore, this type of happiness cannot counteract negative mental states and actions, and may in fact cause negative attitudes. For this reason, Buddha labels this kind of happiness the 'suffering of change.' He never said it was entirely suffering. He said it was superficial happiness, a facsimile, and therefore must not be pursued as if it were genuine. In the Sutra he defined suffering of change as 'happiness when it arises but suffering when it ceases.' Buddha advised us not to get attached to it because it will necessarily change into suffering. When we ignorantly expect genuine happiness to come from external things — when we put conditions on happiness by thinking that we will be happy only when we get something, and refuse to be happy when we don't — then we are in a state of attachment.

Simply wanting, admiring, aspiring, desiring or wishing for something is not necessarily attachment. A traveler must not, however, fall under the delusion that they own their house when, in fact, they have only checked into a five-star hotel! They are aware of the fact that sooner or later they will have to check out. They can enjoy their luxurious room during their stay, but without developing attachment to it. After leaving their room they don't feel a sense of loss or unhappiness. This could be an indication that they did not develop attachment for it, only admiration and appreciation. Similarly, Buddha did not advocate renouncing temporary happiness, but to enjoy it without attachment, and then to skillfully use it as a basis for engendering lasting happiness which is not only sustainable but genuine, meaningful, and abundantly positive. That is the main theme of this book: to strike a balance in which temporary happiness is pursued as a vessel in which to hold the nectar of lasting happiness.

If we are very attached to something that is bound to change for the worse, we will eventually experience frustration and unhappiness. It is not worth becoming attached to it as if it were genuine and lasting; instead, we should just enjoy it as long as we have it. I also want to clarify that Buddha is not against material accumulation; he is only against attachment and its derivative afflictions such as greed and covetousness because attachment is the chief cause of mental suffering. Mental suffering is the main obstacle to unconditional, lasting happiness. Absence of attachment doesn't necessarily imply a lack of aspiration or desire.

People tend to use the terms attachment, desire, wish, admiration, and aspiration synonymously. I will deal with some of their different nuances in a later chapter. What I mean by the term, 'attachment,' in this context is an afflictive emotion, whereas having a desire, a wish, an aspiration or admiration is not necessarily afflictive.

Temporary happiness is dependent happiness. It is so-called because temporary happiness is necessarily dependent upon physical things, external to our mind. We have to run after physical things to obtain temporary happiness. As we chase them, we encounter many obstacles that hinder our getting them, which in turn results in mental suffering such as anger, jealousy, anxiety, sadness, and so on. It is impossible to control all physical things because they are infinite. Dependent happiness is temporary, non-sustainable, and vulnerable because it is necessarily dependent upon physical things that are impossible to control across the board. Happiness that is dependent upon physical happiness and material objects cannot be sustained.

Take the example of happiness which arises from getting a high-paid job; a dependent happiness. At the time of getting the job we are in seventh heaven; our mind is filled with happiness and contentment. As a result, our body, especially our head, feels light, and our face breaks into a smile. Because of getting the job we are happy, mentally, and our body also feels good. Now the question is, can we sustain this happiness for a long period of time? Perhaps we can, as long as we have the job, which requires that we gain control over many stabilizing factors such as our boss, our colleagues, the company's financial health, the overall economy of the nation, and the economies of other nations, since everything in our current world is interconnected. Even if the job has been stabilized and made 'permanent,' to maintain happiness we need to make sure that suffering doesn't pop up from other factors; so we need to gain control over all other physical things, which is clearly impossible. We cannot obtain lasting, genuine happiness from dependent happiness. The fact that it is dependent upon things other than our mind makes dependent happiness temporary and vulnerable. Is there anyone who has attained lasting happiness by running after material things? No, because gaining control over infinite material objects is impossible. Hence materially-creatable-happiness is bound to limitation by its own nature.

Let us look at the development of temporary happiness, like we experience from going to a nice restaurant where we have a delicious meal. As our hunger subsides, we experience a physical sensation of pleasure and fulfillment, which in turn gives rise to mental pleasure and satisfaction. What we experience is temporary mental happiness based on physical happiness, which is caused by getting the delicious food. If we give in to craving and overeat, our physical happiness transforms into the physical suffering of a stomach-ache! Then, in distress, we take some antacid medicine or go for a long walk. After a while it gets better, but then we ache from the long walk! As a result, we head back home and lie down in bed, which again gives rise to a physical feeling of pleasure which, in turn, gives us mental pleasure and satisfaction. Looking at all these twists and turns we find that dependent happiness arises as a result of obtaining material objects, but then gradually changes into suffering. Again, we try to overcome it by acquiring another physical object, which leads to a temporary cessation of the previous suffering, which again gives rise to temporary physical and mental happiness. These will again gradually decline into suffering, propelling us into an endless struggle to dispel suffering and pursue happiness.

In chasing temporary, dependent, superficial happiness with which we are so familiar, notice that we leave our mind completely out of it (without so much as inquiring about it) while trying everything else: chasing, acquiring, creating, controlling material things. As long as we maintain *this* 'status quo' we can never attain the lasting happiness we seek. It is because of this that our happiness is only temporary and conditional, and cannot be utilized as a basis for lasting, and genuine happiness.

We are preoccupied with materially-creatable-happiness and pursue it because it is relatively easy to acquire. Is this wrong? No. There is nothing wrong with it as long as we don't expect it to become lasting happiness; assume that it is the only kind of happiness; or give up trying to go beyond it. We seldom pursue the lasting happiness that cannot be created by material things because we don't know it is possible. There is hope and a way; it is worth giving it a try! That is why I am writing this book.

LASTING HAPPINESS

Put simply, lasting happiness is a happiness that can be sustained at all times. Here, I will introduce lasting happiness from the perspective of its attributes or qualities rather than from a subjective viewpoint, because understanding it when we have not experienced it (which is the case for many of us) can only be through its attributes. Based on these, easily understood synonyms of this type of happiness are 'genuine happiness,' 'reliable happiness,' 'non-dependent happiness,' 'materially-non-creatable happiness,' and 'unconditional happiness.'

Lasting happiness is genuine because it will not deceive us by eventually turning into suffering. It is reliable because it is sustainable. It is skillful because it can transform adversity to advantage. It is strong because it is not vulnerable to problems. It is honest because it will not draw us into harmful actions. It is inexhaustible because sharing it does not deplete its potency. It is unbiased and inclusive because it can be attained by anyone who possesses that beautiful phenomenon called 'mind' and the mental factor of 'feelings.'

Lasting happiness is not dependent upon physical happiness and physical objects; rather, it can be born within our own mind. Its development does not require chasing after physical objects; hence, it is sustainable. Our own mind can be an inexhaustible source of lasting happiness if it is developed, trained, and used correctly.

The uniqueness of lasting happiness lies in the fact that the more we withdraw it from the savings account of our mind, the greater its supply! It is like having a machine at home that prints money: we can print as much as we want without going out for work! Our mind becomes the safest bank and lasting happiness, the best currency! Now, what do you think is the best investment? Would Warren Buffet have the answer?

One of the attributes of lasting happiness is the fact that it is not materially creatable. You can't bribe anyone for it; it is not corruptible. You may be able to buy coffee if you're thirsty, a nice meal if you're hungry, a house if you're homeless; but when it comes to lasting happiness, it can't be just bought with material things. Otherwise, all rich people would already have lasting happiness!

To get a glimpse of it from an empirical first person viewpoint, recall any situation or experience you had in the past when you were simply happy, deep down inside, without having been stimulated by any outer physical thing. It could be a time when your mind became absorbed in a deep breathing exercise, or you engaged in an act of kindness to a stranger, or you looked at your child or parents and genuinely wished them to be happy, and never have suffering befall them. In these experiences one could have a glimpse of lasting happiness.

Getting a glimpse of lasting happiness and truly experiencing it are two distinct aspects. Our initial glimpse needs to be enhanced through systematic mind training to transform it into genuine, lasting happiness. Once when I was en route to Madrid from Barcelona on the fast train I was seated in the middle chair between two very reserved gentlemen dressed in full suits and ties. Since I had woken up very early that morning and rushed to the station, I hadn't had my regular coffee, and so I had a slight headache and body ache. Given the serene silence in the train compartment I thought to myself, why not just meditate for the duration of the trip? which was about 3 hours. I gently reclined my seat trying not to disturb the two men who didn't seem at all interested in striking up a conversation with me. I started the meditation by just being aware of my bodily feelings, particularly the heaviness in my head and body. Then I gradually shifted to focusing on my breathing. I alternated between these two and made sure that my awareness remained clear and alert without falling asleep. As I did this, I could feel the pain in my head and body receding and being replaced by a blissful feeling. Then, about fifteen minutes later, I suddenly felt a tap on my shoulder and heard, 'Hola, Hola!' (Hello in Spanish). The gentleman on my right wanted to get out, and as I looked out the window, I realized that I had already arrived in Madrid! I wished I hadn't arrived so soon, thus interrupting my glimpse of lasting happiness!

When I was studying at Tibetan Children Village school as a young child, I frequently found myself filled with curiosity and wonder about what was happening behind my hostel which was nestled halfway up a mountain. Mountains rose from there up to the snowcaps of the Himalayas. There was a barbed wire fence several meters behind our hostel. Barely 14, I was warned not to cross that fence or I would receive a demerit which could lead to severe punishment. One day I gathered courage, leaned under the fence, and crossed to the other side. I slowly climbed to the summit of the mountain where there was a small valley. Continuing down the valley I came across a beautiful small lawn with four jam bottles filled with water stuck in the ground. There were beautiful birds sipping water from them. At the left corner of the lawn was a small hut with a gate made from a wooden beam. On it were written the words, 'kindly do not disturb.' I quietly raised the beam and walked inside. The hut had a mesh door and I couldn't see through it. I raised my voice and said "Anybody there?" Suddenly a voice came from within, "What do you want?" I replied, "I want teachings on Dharma!" The reply came back, "Come on in!" So I opened the door. Before me was a majestic and serene looking monk with a joyous smile, seated in a cross-legged position. He introduced himself as Gen Lamrimpa Jamphel Tenzin.

I immediately made three prostrations and sat near him. "Okay, so you want teachings on Buddha Dharma?" he asked. I replied "Yes." "What kind of teaching?" I said, "I don't know, whatever you think might be suitable for me." He handed me a small text entitled 'Lamrim, Stages of the Path to Liberation" and told me that we would start with teaching based on that. He said, "But before teaching, let's have tea," and he made some on a small kerosene stove using Nestle milkmaid. The tea was so delicious, even better than the tea served at my school. He asked me to come the next day in the afternoon since his mornings and evenings were reserved for his meditation sessions. The teaching from him continued for several days until I was finally caught climbing through the fence and given one demerit. Getting three demerits would mean expulsion from the school. During one of the teachings on lamrim there was a section about the sufferings of sentient beings of the six migrations: three happy migrations which included humans, demi-gods, and gods, and three unhappy migrations which included hells, animals, and hungry ghosts. After contemplating these sufferings, I was supposed to meditate on compassion in the form of wishing beings to be free from suffering. After the teachings, as I made my way back to the hostel, I noticed two Indian men engaged in an activity near a tree. As I approached closer, I realized they were slaughtering a white lamb that was tied to the tree. Witnessing this incident deeply affected me, leaving me unable to engage in meditation for several days. Then one day in the classroom, I was bored of the subject and went into a dark room, sort of a walk-in closet, that was connected to the classroom. I sat there in the dark while the class continued. I meditated on the sufferings of the animal realm based on the lamrim text, wishing them to be free from sufferings, but it was kind of dry, not very emotionally moving. Then I recalled the incident when the poor lamb was being slaughtered. I remembered the animal's suffering in minute, vivid detail, and suddenly I felt strong compassion, got goose-bumps, with tears running down my face. But at the same time, I felt great peace and a blissful feeling that filled my entire body and mind. I had never felt such bliss in my life and was quite surprised that, instead of feeling fear, I felt great bliss. I think this must have been my first glimpse of lasting happiness. It couldn't develop into actual lasting happiness at that time but, nevertheless, a mere glimpse of lasting happiness is a blessing. The next day I reported this experience to my teacher, Gen Lamrimpa, and he recounted a similar experience he had had in Tibet when he was young. While meditating in his cave during the winter the surroundings were filled with white snowflakes, temperatures below zero. He was meditating on the sufferings of cold hell beings. Although he was following all the meditative steps, it was not evoking much of an emotional response. So he took very drastic steps: he prepared hot water and a warm blanket, then went outside in the snow with only a loincloth. He sat cross-legged in the snow for about 15 minutes, then finally came back into his cave, wrapped himself in a blanket, and drank his hot water. He almost died. But since then, he was able to meditate very successfully on the sufferings of cold hell beings. Gen Lamrimpa also commented that the reason I felt profound bliss instead of fear is that the compassion I cultivated through meditation was pure. Within Lamrim, there is a section about the Four Noble Truths which Gen Lamrimpa elucidated so beautifully that I became fascinated by the third noble truth, "The noble truth of the cessation of suffering."

Milarepa, Tibet's renowned yogi, was materially one of the poorest of people, but he was one of the happiest because he attained the highest degree of lasting happiness. Just living in his cave, he was able to derive immense happiness from no other source than his own mind, which was always accessible to him, just as ours is to us.

Of course, this does not mean that we should all confine ourselves to caves and drop out! Whether we are materially prosperous or not, we can apply ourselves to inner development just as Milarepa did. What we need to do is strike a balance between temporary and lasting happiness in order to make our life happier and more meaningful. If humanity veers away from this delicate balance and persists in relentlessly pursuing fleeting, short-term happiness without considering the broader consequences, the future may bring a grave outcome: our beloved Mother Earth becoming uninhabitable due to the adverse effects of climate change, caused primarily by human activities. Striking a balance in which temporary happiness is pursued as a foundation to engender lasting happiness is truly a noble endeavor.

We shouldn't deprive ourselves of the opportunity to realize lasting happiness simply because we are pursuing temporary happiness, and vice-versa. The key is to view temporary happiness as a stepping stone, rather than the ultimate goal. Lasting happiness, as a long-term aspiration can be realized by anyone who can train their mind through learning, contemplation and meditation. Don't get trapped by outdated patterns that have proven to be ineffectual. Instead, discover new approaches and embrace being a true explorer. All living beings are eligible for this.

If we could attain lasting happiness, given the definition above, it would truly be good, perfect, and precious. The important question now is: Can we actually realize this beautiful and perfect happiness, or is it just a fantasy that is too good to be true? This question is crucial because any goal, no matter how noble, is meaningless if it is unattainable. Are the positive qualities attributed to lasting happiness possible, or are they merely projections of fantasy?

To answer this question, we must embark on a journey into the inner realms of our minds to explore the potential for attaining lasting, materially-non-creatable-happiness. We need to understand that the goal we are pursuing is not just an ideal, but an actual possibility within our reach; otherwise, our efforts may prove futile. Recognizing the feasibility of such happiness, and understanding that we can take actions towards achieving it, imbues us with confidence and provides a perspective on life's meaning.

Finding meaning in life is one of the paths to experiencing lasting happiness. This type of enduring happiness isn't solely about sensory stimulation; it delves deeper, encompassing feelings of contentment and a sense of purpose. What could be more significant than realizing our innate potential to experience this kind of happiness? Therefore, to generate this meaningful perspective and to 'kickstart' our inward journey, we must first logically and reasonably establish that lasting happiness is within the realm of possibility.

WHY LASTING HAPPINESS IS POSSIBLE?

We have all experienced physical and mental happiness at one time or another in our lives. These have, unfortunately, been temporary and often unsatisfactory. So we are now searching for genuine, lasting happiness. There are two possible sources from which we may try to derive lasting happiness. These are the material realm and the mental realm. Out of these two, we have sought much happiness in the material realm, yet all we have obtained is a mixed bag of temporary happiness followed by a lot of suffering. It is clear that we cannot acquire lasting happiness from physical objects because that would require gaining control of them all, which is not possible. Nor can we engender lasting happiness from the mental realm as long as we remain in our current state of mind, which I also call our 'default mind.' It is marked by the fact that we let ourselves be controlled by our mind, which is in turn controlled by physical things. As long as this continues, we end up with only dependent happiness, which is superficial and temporary.

Once we exclude material objects and our current mental state as the source of lasting happiness, the only alternative left is to train and transform our mind. We need to take care of our own mind and then let our mind take care of everything else, including material things. We cannot control the infinite material world but we can control our subjective experience of it.

In order to engender lasting happiness, we must do something with our own mind; that is the only possibility. We human beings, and animals as well, have used our minds to deal with physical things, i.e., objects other than our own minds, creating, controlling, modifying, acquiring and manipulating them. Rarely have we used our mind to take care of itself. The result is that we end up experiencing only temporary happiness accompanied by many problems and much suffering. We have been like a bad employer who hires someone to do all sorts of work but gives them no training at all, pays them very little, and gives them no benefits! Hence the mind as an employee becomes unproductive, produces only temporal happiness, and hides genuine happiness.

Up to now our approach has not worked to engender lasting happiness. Therefore, if we aspire for such happiness, we must alter our strategy and adopt a new methodology. Hoping for a different outcome while employing the same approach would be akin to 'insanity'. Given that controlling material objects and maintaining our current mental state hasn't brought lasting happiness, we should consider a different path: training our minds so that we can direct them freely. This way, our minds will be under our control, rather than controlling us!

Is it possible to experience lasting happiness by training our mind? Is lasting happiness too good to be true? To gain perspective on this million-dollar question and find a convincing answer, we must explore it for ourselves; not the material world — which we have been doing to our own exhaustion! — but the inner universe, the world of our mind, which we have not yet explored. Just as the external world brims with wonders like beautiful landscapes decorated with rivers, lakes, mountains, and islands, the exploration of the inner universe of our minds can also lead to deep insights and discoveries. In this exploration, we may even stumble upon the most precious treasure, one that is comparable to water. Water is vital to our existence, yet so simple that we often forget to appreciate it and drink it. The greatest secret we all possess is also simple, residing in our own mind— yet we seldom even acknowledge its existence, much less appreciate it!

If we can investigate the workings of our inner world and discover how it operates, this will determine whether or not we can answer that million-dollar question. There is no direct and simple answer to the question "Is lasting happiness possible?" It is critical to do this exploration for ourselves because it may convince us whether or not lasting happiness *is* possible. To gain such conviction we must understand the process by which lasting happiness arises and a method which can lead to it.

There are different levels of lasting happiness that we can experience, ranging from basic to the highest level. The basic level of lasting happiness can be sustained throughout this lifetime, whereas higher levels of lasting happiness can extend to future lives; in other words, they can transcend time. The basic level of lasting happiness is attainable by anyone regardless of their religious affiliation, or lack thereof. The highest level of lasting happiness is Great Nirvana, which many may not have considered pursuing. At the end of this book, I will briefly describe the process of attaining Great Nirvana, not necessarily as a targeted goal, but in order to gain the conviction that it may be possible; even this can give us great joy and a sense of true meaning in our lives. Imagine the impact it would have if you could become fully convinced, not through blind faith, but through reasoning and personal experience, that the highest level of lasting happiness is within reach for everyone. How would this influence you? Perhaps we could aspire to remove words like "self-destructive" and "suicidal" from our dictionary, as this understanding opens up new realms of hope and possibility.

The mere hope of the possibility of Nirvana has fascinated me, even from a very young age. At the age of 14 I was fortunate to have met Gen Lamrimpa, a hermit meditator who lived in the mountains above our school. I had crossed the boundary line of the school, just a barbed wire fence, many times to receive teachings from Gen Lamrimpa. Thanks to his excellent teachings, particularly on the concepts of the Four Noble Truths, and probably my own spiritual karma, I developed a great admiration for Nirvana, becoming so fascinated by it that I took its pursuit very seriously. I also felt that Nirvana could only be achieved through lifelong, dedicated meditation practice like my teacher, Gen Lamrimpa, was doing. For me, Gen Lamrimpa embodies the concept of Nirvana as he explained it: a state in which all afflictions are ceased, and there is no more suffering of illness, aging, death, and so on. This led me to have a strong aspiration to become a hermit meditator, *'jadrel'* in Tibetan, one who renounces mundane activities. I shared this aspiration with my friends and teacher at school but they all laughed and didn't take me seriously. For them, giving up all mundane activities and meditating in a cave seemed unimaginable. Nevertheless, my aspiration, whether it was genuine or mere fantasy, was very real to me and gave me lots of hope and a sense of meaningfulness to my life. Then, one day, a thought arose in me to write a letter to His Holiness the Dalai Lama, himself, seeking his guidance about my aspiration for nirvana. My friend, Sonam Wangchen, and I, who shared a similar yearning, sent the letter.

To our surprise, His Holiness not only replied but also summoned us. A few days after sending the letter, our school principal called us to his office and informed us that we were summoned by the Private Office of HH Dalai Lama for an audience with His Holiness. Never in my wildest dreams did I think we would receive a response, let alone a private audience. We were nervously excited about this unexpected opportunity. We were to meet with His Holiness in three days. The news spread like wildfire through the school, and we became the talk of the town. Everybody started to take us seriously, and congratulate us even before the audience occurred. In 1991, to a Tibetan, securing a private audience with His Holiness the Dalai Lama was akin to winning the lottery. To a non-Tibetan, His Holiness might be seen as a simple Buddhist monk, but for a Tibetan, he is a living Buddha– meeting him was like encountering Jesus Christ in the flesh for a Christian.

On the third morning, dressed in traditional Tibetan attire called "chuba," we were escorted on foot by the principal himself to His Holiness's private residence. It took nearly an hour. Once we arrived, we were admitted to a spacious verandah where a security check took place. After clearance, we entered an office with a large glass wall overlooking a beautiful garden. A big wooden brown table and office chair were present. After a few minutes, His Holiness entered and took a seat. We promptly performed three prostrations and presented traditional scarves to receive his blessings. Seated on the floor near him, we gazed upward at his compassionate face, which resembled a descending sun radiating rays of hope and compassion. His Holiness inquired about our school life, studies, and favorite subjects. He then asked how we developed aspirations to become hermit meditators, *jadrel*, and what had inspired us. I recounted my encounter with Gen Lamrimpa and receiving teachings on Lamrim and the Four Noble Truths. His Holiness remarked, "Though your aspirations are wholesome, one cannot simply venture into the forest to meditate. It requires thorough preparation. Buddha's teachings are divided into two categories: Sutrayana and Tantrayana. Within Sutrayana, there are four Buddhist tenet systems, and one must study the first three before delving into the fourth. The tenets of the fourth system, especially with respect to the ultimate mode of nature, *shunyat*a, must be studied and understood." Regarding Tantrayana, I recall his rocket analogy: even though tantra can lead to Nirvana very quickly, it requires a skilled pilot, like an astronaut. After explaining these concepts, he proposed that we study Buddhism comprehensively before becoming *jadrel*. To achieve this, we could either join one of the three great monasteries in South India or his private monastery, *Namgyal Dratsang*. In the latter scenario, His Holiness would even assign a private teacher to guide us. Before concluding our audience, His Holiness reached into one of the drawers on the table and retrieved a sachet containing a precious Mani pill. Using his fingers, he extracted several pills and extended his hand towards us. I instinctively reached out to receive it, but he kindly gestured for us to open our mouths and dropped the pills directly into them. Such a compassionate gesture not only validated my nirvana aspiration but also opened my spiritual path in ways I could never have imagined. I will remain forever grateful and indebted for this profound experience. While Nirvana itself has eluded me and still seems quite far away, nevertheless, Nirvana wisdom, blessed by His Holiness, has taken root within me, and continually evolved ever since. It has been a bountiful source of strength, hope, a sense of meaning in life, and a profound level of happiness. Hence, I sincerely hope that, as your tour guide, I can take you on this inner journey and offer each of you with a meaningful glimpse of Nirvana wisdom. So please join me!

WHY LASTING HAPPINESS IS POSSIBLE?

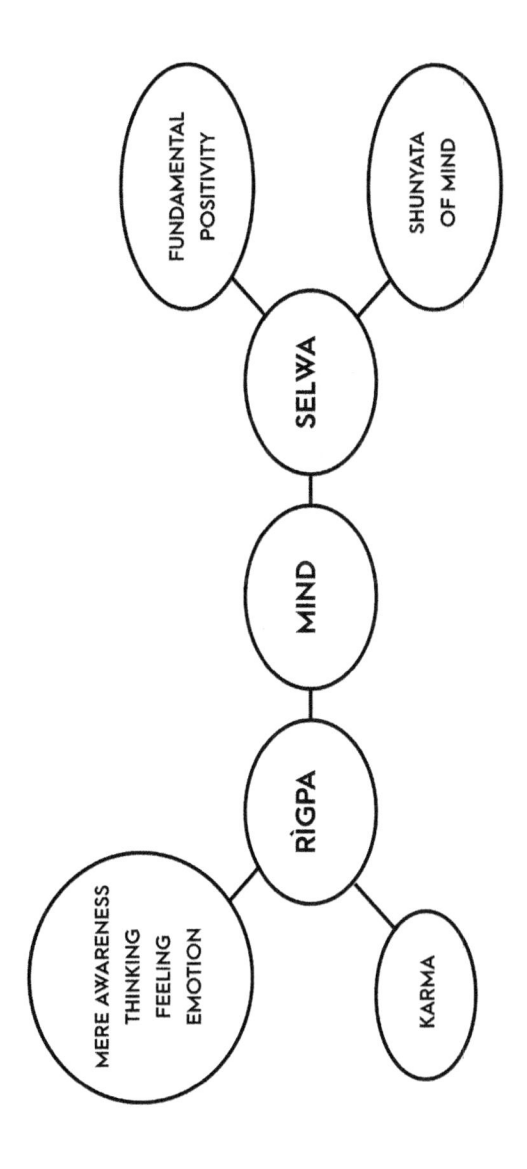

```
        FUNDAMENTAL        SHUNYATA
         POSITIVITY         OF MIND
                \         /
                 \       /
                  SELWA
                    |
                   MIND
                    |
                  RIGPA
                  /    \
                 /      \
   MERE AWARENESS      KARMA
   THINKING
   FEELING
   EMOTION
```

(fig.1)

Now, let us begin our daring exploration! We begin by first introducing a new world: 'mind.' Are you ready? Here we go!

31

MIND, OUR NEW WORLD

All of us are sentient beings because we have this unique thing called a 'mind'. Mind is the most wonderful thing in the universe. It sets us apart from inanimate things. It enables us to experience happiness and suffering. In the following discussion, I will delve into the Buddhist perspective on the nature of the mind, drawing from both the teachings of the Buddha and my personal experiences.

Buddha's definition of mind is very simple. It has two attributes: *'Selwa'* and *'Rigpa.'* The Tibetan terms *Selwa* means clarity, the fundamental entity of mind, and *Rigpa* means knowing, the fundamental function of mind. The great Indian Buddhist master Dharmakirti (6th C.) puts it beautifully: "Since all obscurations are adventitious the nature of mind is luminous and clear." Luminosity refers to *Rigpa*, the knowing, reflecting function of mind. Clarity or clearness refers to *Selwa*, the fundamental nature of mind.

Indeed, the term *"Rigpa"* encompasses a multitude of facets when it comes to knowing. It can manifest in various forms such as mere awareness, or reflection, perception, understanding, thinking, discernment, aspiration, feeling, emotional experience, and more. If we stop for a moment and turn inwards, look at our mind and feel what it does, we can understand what *Rigpa* means.

Strings of words and sentences in this book appear to you and you perceive them and discern their meanings, generating corresponding thoughts based on them. Then you may develop emotions and feelings of some kind. That is your *Rigpa* in operation. *Rigpa* is like the function of a crystal mirror, reflecting anything that comes before it. Mind can reflect, perceive, know, understand, discern, think, imagine, remember, manifest emotionally, and 'feel' its relation to any object. Thus, mind is a vast umbrella encompassing many different mental factors. The understanding of mind should not be confined to 'thoughts' or 'thinking mind' as many people do in the west. Amongst all these different mental factors, it is actually the ability to 'imagine' and 'feel' that I consider the most important.

From these defining characteristics we can understand that mind includes many different varieties: sensory mind, conceptual mind, non-conceptual mind, thinking mind, imaginative mind, feeling mind, emotional mind, memory mind, gross mind, subtle mind and subtlest mind. Thus, 'mind' is not confined to analytical thought related with the brain; rather, it has many aspects. Both negative mind, which is the cause of all suffering, and buddha-mind, which is completely pure and immaculate, are minds. Both equally possess the two attributes of clarity and awareness. From the standpoint of their fundamental natures, the mind of Buddha and the mind of ordinary beings are the same. The difference is that the *Selwa* of ordinary beings is temporarily obscured by negativity, whereas the *Selwa* of buddha-mind is free of all negativity and obscuration. The phenomenon that possesses the qualities of clarity *(Selwa)* and knowing *(Rigpa)* is defined as mind.

Selwa is the essential nature of the mind and constitutes the greatest secret; so much so that Buddha focused his career on revealing it. Out of the three wheels of Dharma that he turned, the second and third are dedicated to revealing *Selwa*. It is said, "Whoever understands *Selwa* understands Buddha's teachings!"

The very nature of the mind is clear in the sense that the negativities, including their mastermind—root negativity, which obscure our mind, are temporary and adventitious.

Our mind has many negative aspects but these cannot penetrate its very nature and become an intrinsic part of it. It is like a crystal mirror covered by a black cloth. Since the very nature of the mind is not polluted by negativity; it is in the nature of 'clarity' *(Selwa)*. A crystal mirror is very clear, and black cloth obscures it only temporarily. Any object that comes before a crystal mirror is reflected in it. The natural clarity of a crystal mirror and its ability to reflect objects is metaphorically similar to mind's nature of clarity *(Selwa)* and its function of knowing *(Rigpa)*.

Thus, the definition of mind is simple. These characteristics pervade all minds and vice-versa — 'mind' pervades these characteristics. The metaphor is easily understandable: the crystal mirror is clear and the cloth obscures it only temporarily. However, applying this example to the actuality of our mind, clarity *(Selwa)* with temporary obscuration, is not easy to comprehend. How and why is negativity not in the nature of our mind, even though it exists in our mind? How does positive potential exist in the very nature of our mind? We need a reasonable explanation for this. These are the most important questions human beings have asked, and all of Buddha's teachings can be summarized as answers to them. I will present these answers in the later chapter, *Selwa* (Clarity).

Mind can also be categorized into four divisions based on their subtlety – very gross mind, gross mind, subtle mind and subtlest mind. Subtlest mind is similar to what we term 'spirit' or 'soul' in the west and is known as 'clear light mind' in the Buddhist tantric system. Sensory consciousnesses such as sight are examples of very gross mind. Our normal thinking and discernment is gross mind. Most of our emotions and feelings are also gross minds, even though there are also feelings and emotions that are subtle and subtlest minds. People in deep sleep and coma do not have gross feelings and emotions but they do have feelings and emotions that are subtle and subtlest minds. Our normal waking mind is a gross mind but it can be refined, enhanced and transformed into a subtler mind through meditation. Our gross mind can reach a point where it is very stable and clear; stable in the sense that it can focus on any chosen object single-pointedly, and clear in the sense that it can perceive objects with intense clarity, just as if they were seen by the eyes. When our gross mind reaches this state, it has transformed into a subtle mind.

Subtlest mind comes from infinite time past and keeps going for infinite time into the future. This mind is our innermost, pure, immaculate mind, similar to the mind of a Buddha. It is like the nuclear force within atoms— very powerful if correctly tapped into, but otherwise tiny and ineffectual. We all have a subtlest mind but it remains dormant as long as our subtle, gross, and very gross minds are functioning. Subtlest mind only manifests naturally for a short period of time during deep sleep, sexual climax, sneezing, and at the final moment of death when all other gross and subtle minds have ceased. Methods to manifest and utilize this subtlest mind, however, can be found only in the Buddhist systems of Tantra. This subtlest mind, also called clear-light-mind, is most powerful but also difficult to get control of. The energy-wind associated with it, which moves this clear-light-mind to its object, is the most powerful physical matter according to Buddhist Tantra. It is the basis for developing an illusory body, called *Gyulu* in Tibetan, an indestructible form which frees us from the cyclic existence of death and rebirth.

In Tibetan society, we have many senior monks who, when clinically dead, enter into a meditative state called *Thuktham*. During this state, monks exhibit certain signs such as the body maintaining vitality as if alive, absence of decomposing smell even after several weeks, heat at the point of heart, and maintaining the meditative posture even after rigor mortis has passed or has not occurred in the first place, among others. Unlike ordinary people, where the subtlest mind exists the body very quickly after death, these monks are able to control the subtlest mind and prevent it from leaving the body. Despite being clinically dead, they can exhibit these signs due to the abiding of the subtlest mind still in their body. I have personally witnessed two such instances in the monastery.

In this Book of Happiness, we shall not concern ourselves very much with the subtlest mind because it is virtually non-existent during our life, and we have little control over it. We will focus more on the gross mind because it is what is functioning during our normal life, and it is relatively easier to control. In addition, the more we can direct our gross mind, the more this will impact our subtle and subtlest mind. The more we train our gross mind, the less we will be controlled by it, and the closer we will come to our subtle mind. The closer we come to our subtle mind, the greater role it will play in our daily life. This is good because subtle mind is more powerful than gross mind for providing happiness and creativity. In this book, however, we will mainly deal with gross mind and its transformation to subtler mind through meditation.

Many spiritual advisors advocate shunning or stopping the gross mind of thought. I strongly disagree and recommend that we never just shun the gross mind, but engage it and deal with it. It is a beauty of meditation that, by skillfully utilizing thought, concepts can become more subtle and dissolve like sticks rubbed together igniting and eventually consuming themselves. The only moment when we can let go of thoughts and discourage the thinking process is during the initial phase of our meditation process when we 'return to the fundamental nature of mind.' At that moment, we observe things as they are, using mere awareness without resorting to deeper thinking and contemplation. The objects of mere awareness tend to be things like physical sensations, feelings, emotions, and breathing, because these are vivid enough to evoke mere awareness. If a phenomenon is not sufficiently vivid, being more abstract in nature, our mind tends to venture beyond mere awareness, engaging in deeper thinking and projection.

When we are conceived in the womb, mind first arises as subtlest mind, then as subtle mind, then as gross mind, and finally as very gross mind. All these levels of mind have the fundamental attributes of clarity and awareness. Different minds have different aspects, potentials, and qualities, but they all share these attributes in common. Therefore, negative mind has a negative aspect and potential, but since it is 'mind' it is still 'clarity' and awareness; and since it is clarity by nature, it is not inherently negative. This implies that negativity can be removed from it, just as black cloth can be removed from a crystal mirror.

All other levels of mind emerge from the subtlest mind. It is the base from which the subtle, gross and very gross minds emerge. When very gross and gross minds are functioning, subtle and subtlest mind remain inactive.

RIGPA

According to the teachings of the Buddha, all phenomena, both internal and external, originate from the mind. *Rigpa* plays a crucial role in this process by allowing objects to first appear within the mind's field of mere awareness. The mind then engages in perceiving, thinking, knowing, and understanding these objects, albeit not always in a completely accurate manner. Subsequently, feelings and emotions arise based on the interaction between the mind and its objects. Whether these feelings are pleasant, unpleasant, or neutral depends on the nature of that interaction. Our mind serves as the mechanism and medium through which we establish our understanding and experience of everything. Without the mind, nothing would exist. It is through the mind's engagement with the world that our reality is constructed. This understanding highlights the profound influence our mind has in shaping our perception, interpretation, and emotional response to the external and internal aspects of our existence.

There is yet another significant manner in which the mind gives rise to all phenomena: through the principle of karmic causality. I will elaborate on this concept in due course. As previously mentioned, the innate desire for happiness is inherent in all sentient beings. This desire is made possible by our capacity to experience feelings. *Rigpa,* being the source of feeling, holds great significance in this context. The function of feeling within the mind is of utmost importance, as all beings strive to attain as much happiness as possible. Without the ability to feel, happiness would lose its meaning entirely.

Consequently, we can categorize minds based on the diverse functions that arise from *Rigpa*:

- Sensory mind
- Conceptual mind
- Cognitive mind
- Memory mind
- Emotional mind
- Feeling mind

Sensory Mind

Sensory mind is an awareness which perceives any of five sense objects – sights, sounds, smells, tastes and tactile objects, in reliance upon the sense organs. There are five sensory minds: eye awareness, ear awareness, nose, tongue and body awareness. These are very gross minds because whenever they arise, we can immediately recognize them. The objects which stimulate them and the five sense powers upon which they depend, are all physical entities. The five sensory minds are unique in their functions, in that the eye can only see color and shape but not sound, smell, taste etc. The ear can hear sounds but not color, shapes, smells, etc. The same applies to nose, tongue and body awarenesses. However, according to the Buddhist tantric system, a meditator can utilize his energy-winds in such a way that all five sensory minds become interchangeable in their functions. In that case, the eye can see not only colors and shapes, but other objects of smell, sound, taste, and touch, as well. The same goes for the other senses, and not just nearby objects but all objects throughout the universe. The body awareness, for example, can feel not only what it has touched, but all tactile objects in the universe without having to have physical contact. This raises ethical issues, however, because a tantric practitioner can physically interact with every person in the universe!

Conceptual Mind

Conceptual mind, or thinking mind, is an awareness which thinks about or analyzes an object, be it real or imagined. All the infinite phenomena can be the object of a thinking mind. The thinking ability of the human mind makes us unique compared to other species. It can be destructive, causing suffering, but can also be constructive by bringing about happiness; we have both of these possibilities. Animals, on the other hand, have less mental suffering due to less thinking ability, but they also have less possibility for attaining happiness, especially lasting happiness. Animals must take human rebirth in order to realize lasting happiness. That is why Buddha says that human life is very precious, so precious that we should not waste it by seeking only temporary happiness. Rather, we should make best use of it for developing lasting happiness. This involves not only taking care of this life but also considering the well-beings of infinite lives that follows after.

Initially our thinking mind primarily engages in conceptual thought. Through consistent meditation, however, there is a way to transform gross conceptual mind into subtle non-conceptual mind.

Conceptual mind comprehends objects indirectly, by way of a mental image. Whenever we think about something, we mentally construct a picture using a name, and through this mental picture we reflect on it. Because of this, the mental image becomes a kind of barrier between the object and our mind, and its name becomes a barrier between the mental image and our mind. But the mental image initially serves as a medium through which we can perceive and think about the object. Without going through this process, there is no way that we can understand an object. Even though the mental image is not the actual object, it is a valid medium through which the conceptual mind can perceive it.

Suppose we are looking for our car key. Our conceptual mind has a mental image of the key, and when we finally see it lying at a corner of a bookshelf, we realize that this is the key. Had we not possessed a mental image of the key, we would not have found the key even when we see it on the shelf. Later if we destroy the key by grinding it into powder, we would still have the mental image of the key even though it no longer exists. This shows that the mental image of the key is not the actual key and vice-versa. This is easily established when the object is a material object such as a key, but when it is a non-physical abstract concept such as impermanence, goodness, badness and so on, it is difficult to differentiate between the object and its mental image. Only through meditative experience can they be differentiated.

When conceptual mind apprehends an object, it does so by way of a mental image as if the object and the image were one. During the process of analytical meditation, a meditator repeatedly focuses upon a chosen object. It is conceptual thought which is being used for this. Sense consciousnesses cannot meditate.

Emotions and feelings occur more as resultant states, with conceptual thought operating as their cause. Therefore, if you would like more control over your feelings and emotions you should direct your thoughts wisely, because they are their causes. Meditation initially works more with causal thought than its resultant feelings and emotions. Dealing with things at the causal stage is more effective in the long run. There is a point, however, when feelings and emotions can be worked with directly through mindfulness meditation.

To summarize the process, initially we must meditate using our conceptual mind. As we meditate on our chosen object, we do so by way of a mental image of the object. Even though perceiving the object in this way is valid, the mental image obscures the mind from seeing its object clearly and becomes a barrier between the two. This barrier induces a dualistic experience – it seems as if our mind and its object are separate. This sense of separateness creates distance between our mind and its object, making it difficult to connect and merge the two. That is why meditation does not seem to transform the mind at first. As we meditate more and more, however, transformation will take place, gradually and steadily. We must be patient and persevering when it comes to meditation. Once transformation takes place as a result of meditation, the mind will become stable and reliable.

As we continually meditate on an object by way of its mental image, the mental image gradually diminishes while the actual object becomes clearer. Then we reach a point when the mind seems to penetrate its object and become one with it. Continuing our meditation, as the mental image diminishes more and more, the barrier of dualistic appearance and experience gradually fades to a point where our mind does not feel that there is an external object being comprehended, only a subjective mind comprehending it. At this stage, the gross level of dualistic experience and appearance has been eliminated. Nevertheless, there is still a subtle dualistic appearance. As we continue meditating on the object, the mental image diminishes even more, the appearance of the actual object becomes even clearer, and the dualistic appearance fades away even further. As a result, we reach a point where we cannot even sense the existence of a subjective mind. The subject and object still appear as dual, but in a very subtle way. It is so subtle that our mind cannot sense that subject and object are appearing to it. Even though there is still a dualistic appearance, there is no longer a dualistic experience. As we meditate still more, the mental image of the object completely dissolves and the actual object appears with vivid clarity. Even subtle dualistic appearance dissipates and our mind touches the object, nakedly and directly, without the mental image. At this point, the transition from conceptual to non-conceptual mind is complete. Our gross mind has transformed into a very subtle mind. The mind merges with its object completely, like water poured into water, and all traces of duality are extinguished.

Cognitive Mind

Cognitive mind is awareness that affirms, projects, and comprehends as a result of thinking and analysis. It draws conclusions from the process of thinking. Depending on how we have thought and analyzed, whether correctly or incorrectly, we will develop one of two kinds of cognitive mind – valid cognition or invalid cognition. Valid cognition cognizes phenomena in accordance with their existence, whereas invalid cognition draws wrong conclusions and misapprehends phenomena. Invalid cognition superimposes the existence of something that does not exist, or exaggerates or denies something that does exist. Valid cognition, being free of such mistakes, can be conceptual or non-conceptual, and is vital to generating lasting happiness. In pursuit of lasting happiness, we will primarily be using our conceptual valid cognition because, at initial stages of meditation, we use conceptual mind to engage in analytical and placement meditation.

Memory Mind

Memory is one of the most important aspects of awareness. It is a link between all of the mental factors. For example, once you have realized something through reasoning you can then remember it without going through the reasoning process again. It connects past mind to present mind through remembrance. It is a latent potential, like an imprint laid down by the mind.

Emotional Mind

In this terminology I am differentiating between feeling and emotion with feelings being *experiences* of pleasure, pain, or neutrality, and emotions being *responses* to those experiences. Emotions are primarily caused by a process in which sensory minds perceive objects, thinking mind analyzes them, and cognitive mind draws conclusions. There are two kinds of emotions: non-afflictive emotions and afflictive emotions; or what we could call positive emotions and negative emotions. Anger, fear, jealousy, worry, anxiety, sadness are some afflictive emotions. Compassion, love, and desire for lasting happiness are examples of non-afflictive emotions.

If we neglect and are oblivious to the workings of our mind, then we will also be neglecting our emotions and feelings. It is not easy or effective to deal with emotions and feelings directly. We must approach them by way of other prior minds, especially thinking and cognitive minds, which induce and influence our feelings and emotions. Meditation is a very powerful tool to directly affect our thinking and cognitive minds, and thereby affect our feelings and emotions.

When a powerful emotion strikes, we cannot help but be overwhelmed by it. The effective way to deal with a negative emotion is to first diminish its force by becoming aware of it; and then let it dissolve into awareness. Once afflictive emotions dissolve, we can use conceptual and cognitive minds to further meditate on them. From the point of view of the mental processes involved, conceptual and cognitive minds are the causal stage when emotions and feelings are developing. If we can bring thinking and cognitive minds under control to direct as we wish, we can diminish and even completely eliminate negative emotions.

Feeling Mind

Feeling mind is a subjective response, an experience. It experiences something as pleasant, unpleasant, or neutral. Emotion, again in this terminology, is a subjective response, a reaction. Emotion and feeling may arise together in a single mind. For instance, when we react angrily, we are emotionally angry and feel unhappy at the same time. Thus, feelings and emotions are related. If we care about our feelings, we should take care of our emotions as well, since positive and negative emotions engender positive and negative feelings. Furthermore, within the sphere of emotions and feelings lies the greatest secret of our mind.

The next stage of our exploration of the inner universe now begins...

MIND IS THE MASTERMIND OF EVERYTHING

While this theme was introduced earlier, its importance warrants a reiteration. Everything, both the external and internal worlds, arises due to the existence of our mind. Without our mind, the world we perceive and experience would simply not exist. *Rigpa,* as the fundamental function of the mind, grants us the ability to perceive, think, reflect, cognize, remember, feel, and emote. These processes give rise to the emergence of feelings and emotions. The nature of these emotional responses, whether positive, negative, or neutral, is dependent upon how our mind interacts with the object in terms of perception, thinking, and understanding. Our mind serves as the medium through which everything is established. Without the mind, our subjective reality would cease to exist. It is akin to a mirror reflecting the multitude of experiences within our consciousness. Remove the mirror, and the reflection dissipates. Through this profound understanding, we underscore the pivotal role our mind plays in shaping our perception, cognition, and emotional experiences, thereby forming the very fabric of our existence.

According to the "observer's effect" of quantum theory, as I understand, mind is not just the medium by which we posit things; it also plays a role in the establishment of the quantum world itself. Mind as an observer can directly influence its observed object. This extraordinary function of mind is only evident when the object is extremely small. I believe that the reason the effect of mind on matter is only evident at the quantum level is because mind's power to influence matter is very subtle. If we enhance the mind's power then its effect on matter can manifest at the macrocosmic level. For example, our mind may be able to move objects just by thinking.

As we age, our face and body undergo momentary changes continuously. Changes take place at the speed of a trillionth of a second, maybe even faster. Buddhism does not assert a shortest moment of time or a smallest particle, because time and mind are infinitely divisible. No matter how much you dissect it, mind retains its fundamental nature and qualities – clarity and awareness. Time, mind, and matter are all infinitely divisible.

The Indian Buddhist master, Dharmakirti (6th C.), posited a shortest moment of time as the time it takes for a smallest particle to flip over; but a smallest particle does not exist in the first place. The change occurring in such a short time cannot be directly observed by our mind because our mind needs a second to function. That is why we cannot observe the aging process in our daily lives. We feel it after many years when changes at the molecular level build up, giving rise to change at the gross level. Buddha called this momentary or transitory nature of reality 'subtle impermanence'.

Our current mind probably cannot complete a task in less than a second. A short standard task for the mind to accomplish, which normally takes about a second, is to perceive a single object like the letter A, or a snap of the fingers. Our mind cannot function in a time frame of 1/100th, 1/1000th or 1/10000th of a second. It needs at least a second to perceive and comprehend an object. When the power of the mind is magnified, however, the time it takes to complete a task decreases. As the power of the mind increases, time slows down correspondingly, and the mind can complete a task in a fraction of a second. Time moves more slowly for an enhanced mind than it does for a normal mind – a billion years to a normal mind can be one year to an enhanced mind. 'An eon can be a second and a second can be an eon,' said the 6th century great Indian Buddhist master, Chandrakirti.

Although our current mind's effect on the physical world is very subtle, that still proves that it has an effect on the material world. It doesn't matter how great or small, an effect is still an effect. When I say 'current mind,' I mean our mind as it is now, not trained or transformed. It is strange that we care so much for our body, our house and other possessions, but never care as much for our mind. This is a kind of betrayal of our mind; it leads to our mind eventually betraying us. Our mind betrays us by not revealing its greatest treasure— the potential to actualize lasting happiness. If we want to discover this treasure in our mind, it is high time that we take care of it, give it due respect, and nourish it, because it is our most precious possession.

MIND IS THE MASTERMIND OF EVERYTHING

Buddha said the same thing centuries ago. It is not mind that is responsible for the many problems that we face individually and globally, it is our untamed and untrained mind. Thought is not to be blamed either; it is our inability to subdue negative thoughts.

Once I was in Glastonbury, England, on a teaching tour, and was invited to a nearby cathedral. I was having a chat with the local priest and said to him, "God must be very pleased with Buddha." Rather surprised, the priest asked, "Why?" I said, 'Among all the creations of God, mind is the most beautiful; and among all people who walked on this earth, Buddha was arguably the finest to reveal its beauty.'

According to recent scientific research, it has become increasingly clear that mind affects the body. Wholesome, relaxed mind, whether thought, emotion or feeling, strengthens the immune system and can have a healing effect. Negative, disturbed mind, be it thought, emotion or feeling, weakens our immune system, leads to ailments, and gives our body no chance to heal. In addition, if you take medicine with a firm belief in its therapeutic potency, it creates a placebo effect that actually contributes to the healing process. According to a recent study, pills that are believed to be more expensive have a higher cure rate than pills a person is told come at a lower price! When our mind believes the pill is expensive, this causes us to believe it is better. The placebo effect is undeniable evidence which demonstrates that our mind affects our body.

Mind affects matter. Mind affects the body. What about the mind itself? Does mind affect itself? Can it affect its various aspects such as gross, subtle and very subtle minds, and its diverse functions such as perceptions, thought, feelings and emotions? The answer is an emphatic, Yes! Mind affects mind in its various aspects even more than it affects physical matter and our bodies.

I will explain this in detail in the chapter, Meditation, Path of the Inner World of Mind. Since our mind serves as the medium by which we perceive, experience, and establish all phenomena, it can be regarded as the mastermind of all existence. Mind's effect on physical matter, the body, and mind itself, points to the fact that mind is the main player. Since every living being has their own mind, they each have a unique inner and external world. Since mind is the mastermind, it would be good if we could control it, because controlling it amounts to controlling everything.

There is another way that mind gives rise to all phenomena; in this, past mind plays a major role. When present mind functions to establish phenomena, it does so in conjunction with past mind; habitual latencies stored within us. Our present mind is conditioned by previous mental action, so it does not have complete freedom in perceiving things and events. The mechanism by which past mind conditions our perceiving, conceiving, emotionalizing, and most importantly, feeling of our inner and outer world, is called 'karma.' This conditioning is especially strong for a mind that is out of control. The more we subdue and transform our mind, the less we will be in bondage of karma. Until we reached the state of Great Nirvana (Buddhahood), we won't be completely free from this bondage.

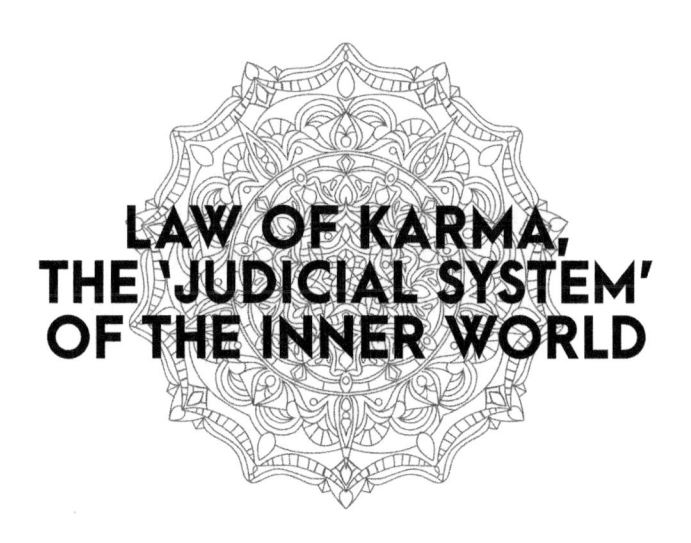

LAW OF KARMA, THE 'JUDICIAL SYSTEM' OF THE INNER WORLD

The natural law of causality pervades all phenomena. It functions in every aspect of our life. Although we can see this to some degree, in certain cases we cannot relate what happens to any tangible cause. In such cases we may simply say it just happened for no reason. The law of karma bridges this gap and makes sense of things and events.

If we look at our body, we see how things work. By exercising, eating balanced food, and maintaining a healthy mind, our body flourishes with vitality. Even a single breath causes a reaction in our body. In the external environment we see the law of causality functioning everywhere. Plants grow because of sun, soil and water. Rain comes from clouds which depend on the evaporation of water. There are many instances and events in our daily lives that demonstrate how causes and conditions bring about effects. If the external world is governed by a law of causality, why not the inner world of our mind?

Karma is action, of which there are three types: physical, verbal, and mental. Of these three, mental karma is the mastermind. Whenever we do something, whether positive or negative, we create karma and this leaves an imprint in our mind; our mind is the storeroom. Don't think we are only accountable for some of our actions; whatever we do makes a difference. The imprints in our mind left by karma eventually ripen and give rise to our future state of being. These imprints also affect the way our current mind functions.

Buddha said that everything comes from causes, and that nothing just happens without cause. If something was causeless it would exist ceaselessly, or it would never exist at all. Since we see that everything around us comes, goes, and changes, it indicates that everything comes from causes. Nothing arises without a cause. Coming from a cause doesn't mean just any cause; it must be a concordant cause, a cause that has the potency to produce it. Everything in our inner and outer worlds comes from a cause and it must be a concordant cause. So, now the big question is, what is a concordant cause?

Of all things that matter to us most, it is our feelings. Without feelings, there is no happiness or suffering. All beings, even an insect, naturally wish for happiness and do not want suffering. From where do feelings of happiness and suffering come? Do they arise without cause? Are they given to us by Buddha as a punishment or reward? Do they arise out of a process of natural selection? Could they arise from any cause whatsoever? None of these four are possible for the following reasons:

1) If feelings (suffering & happiness) came into being without cause, they would continue to exist ceaselessly

LAW OF KARMA

because they would not need any cause to exist. Anything that doesn't depend upon a cause would not need a cause to continue in existence forever. So, why don't feelings of suffering and happiness last forever? Anything that doesn't need a cause to sustain it should have no obstacle to existing forever. With our feelings of suffering and happiness, that is clearly not the case. It is obvious that they come and go.

2) Buddha does not give us feelings of happiness and suffering as rewards and punishment because Buddha has perfect compassion. The main function of perfect compassion is to free all beings from suffering, and to avoid harming them for any reason, whatsoever.

3) The natural selection process, a scientific theory which explains our choices in terms of preserving our survival as a species, only includes a small portion of the law of causality. It does not even pervade the law of karma, much less the entire law of causality.

4) Feelings do not arise from just any cause because, if that were the case, we could be happy no matter what we did. Any action could produce happiness, because anything could be a cause for happiness. If that were the case, we would also have to accept the consequence that we could be happy and sad simultaneously, because anything could cause both happiness and suffering. This is very absurd, indeed.

So, where does happiness and suffering come from? Through the above analysis we can conclude that happiness and suffering arise from causes; not from any cause, but a concordant cause. What is that concordant cause?

To understand this, let's back up for a minute. Everything comes from a cause, and everything has different causes. If you check carefully, all these different causes are either material or mental. The following two analyses show that, ultimately, mind is the root cause of all things.

1) The simultaneous way: it is through mind that we perceive and establish everything. We can even change something if we change the way we perceive it.

2) The causal way: it is through the workings of karma that, when we do something, it lays an imprint in our mind; and this latent but potent imprint eventually ripens, giving rise to things and events we experience around us.

Hence, we can infer that everything is ultimately attributable to the mind. If this assumption holds true, then the mind is the main cause of everything, whether positive, negative, or neutral. Anything contributing to the development of happiness, including happiness itself, falls into the positive category. Conversely, everything that produces or contributes to suffering, including suffering itself, is classified as negative. Neutral feelings and their origins are categorized as neutral. In this way, all things can be categorized as positive, negative, or neutral.

The presumed causal factor, the mind, also encompasses these three aspects: positive, negative, and neutral. Now, if we are given a question in which we have to pair each list of causal factors with its corresponding results, the following scenario would be the closest answer: Positive minds produce positive results, negative minds produce negative results, and neutral minds produce neutral results. This encapsulates the core meaning of the term, 'concordant causes.'

We can confidently assert that positive outcomes originate from positive minds, with no possibility for positive things to be produced by negative or neutral minds. The same applies to negative and neutral things: negative things stem from negative minds, and neutral things come from neutral minds. This aspect is the single most important aspect of the law of karma. If we seek happiness and wish to avoid suffering, we should act in accordance with the law of causality. Pursuing happiness while creating opposite causes will inevitably lead to more suffering and problems.

Buddha said:

"You are your own protector.
If you fully control and train your mind,
You will be liberated to ultimate peace."

SELWA — CLARITY — THE GREATEST SECRET OF MIND

In the previous chapter, it was explained that the fundamental entity of the mind is *Selwa*. *Selwa* is the Tibetan term for clarity, signifying that the nature of the mind is luminous (*Rigpa*) enough to reflect and cognize. Simultaneously, its luminous nature is not inherently obscured by negativities; rather, they are adventitious. Thus, the nature of the mind is characterized by clarity.

Here, clarity primarily refers to how negativities only affect the reflection of phenomena, but do not stain the luminous nature itself. The luminosity remains untouched, as negativities are unable to penetrate and become an inherent part of the mind's luminous nature. The reason for the inability to penetrate into the mind's nature is the presence of something else already occupying the mind's nature, and that is the 'Fundamental Positivity'—the naturally existing positive potential of the mind. Later on, this concept will be explained in detail, as understanding it is crucial for unearthing our greatest secret and experiencing the resulting materially-non-creatable happiness.

The reason why negativities cannot become an inherent part of the mind's nature is due to the emptiness nature of the mind. The mind's emptiness nature, being empty of self-existence in its ultimate manner of existence, makes negativities and their root impossible to be in the nature of the mind.

Not only are negativities adventitious, but they can also be permanently removed by applying the correct antidote. Every religion and system in the world addresses negativity and discusses ways to reduce its impact; however, on a temporary basis. The unique aspect of Buddha's teachings is the emphasis on permanently removing negativity so that it never arises again. This is also made possible by the emptiness nature of the mind.

Hence, *Selwa*—the fundamental nature of the mind—can be understood in two aspects: conventional and ultimate. The mind's naturally existing positive potential (Fundamental Positivity) represents its conventional nature, while the emptiness of the mind represents its ultimate nature. Both of these aspects contribute to the mind's inherent purity and cleanliness, thereby embodying clarity.

Now, what does this mean when our mind is obviously clouded and polluted by negativities? The fact that our mind has obscurations and negativities cannot be denied by anyone. Otherwise, you wouldn't be reading this book about attaining lasting happiness; you would have already attained lasting happiness devoid of all suffering!

Even with the presence of negativities, mind is still clean from the point of view of its fundamental nature. Mind's nature cannot be contaminated by negativities because negativities are not inherent in the nature of the mind. The nature of mind is clear without ever being contaminated by negativities; like water and its nature. When dust is mixed with water, the dust does not mix with the water molecules of hydrogen and oxygen. The dust can be filtered out and separated from the water, but the oxygen molecule cannot. If it is, the water disintegrates and will no longer hold its entity.

Similarly, if negativities were in the nature of the mind, it would not be possible to separate them from the mind. In that case, the only way to destroy negativities would be to destroy the mind. That is not possible. Even if we could destroy the mind, what would be the point? We could not attain lasting happiness, anyway! To experience lasting happiness, we must have feelings, and feeling is a natural part of the mind. Anything that is a natural part of the mind cannot be separated from it. The negativities obscuring our mind do not play any role in making mind what it is; only *Rigpa* and *Selwa* do that. Hydrogen and oxygen make water, not dust; dust only makes the water dirty. Similarly, negativities pollute the mind, but are not an inherent part of it. No matter how strongly they influence the mind, they do not have a permanent place in the mind's own nature. It is like a powerful general who, despite being in command, is not allowed to sit on the throne.

Why are negativities not a natural part of the mind even though they are in it? How is the nature of the mind primordially free from negativity? It is very important to carefully ponder these questions. The answers will determine whether or not our pursuit of lasting happiness is in the realm of possibility.

The primary reason our mind is naturally clean and clear is that negativities have never been able to penetrate and occupy the mind's luminous nature. To demonstrate this, we must establish the fact that positivity, the complete opposite, already occupies the nature of the mind's luminosity. When it comes to the throne of the mind's luminous nature, positivity and negativity cannot coexist.

The naturally existing positive potential of mind successfully prevents negativity from occupying a place within the mind's inherent nature. Negativity and positivity can both exist in our mind, but not in its very luminous nature at the same time. If we can establish that the nature of our mind is naturally positive, this will exclude our mind from being naturally negative. Mind can be negative but only fleetingly, not naturally. Just as the general and the king can both be in the palace at the same time, they cannot occupy the throne simultaneously. If we can prove that the person sitting on the throne is the king, it automatically excludes the person who is not on the throne from being king. Likewise, if we can prove that the nature of mind is positive, it easily leads us to the fact that any negativity in our mind is not our actual nature; it is temporary and can be removed. This understanding sets us on a positive cycle – if positivity is in the nature of the mind, then negativity can't be in its nature. However, since negativity obviously exists, it has to be adventitious and removable, which again leads us back to the fact that the mind is naturally pure.

Another reason why negativity cannot penetrate mind's nature is rooted in the very nature of negativity, itself. Upon examination, we come to realize that all negativities which pollute our mind can be attributed to one root negativity—self grasping mind, and its lieutenant general, self-centered mind. Self grasping mind deputizes self-centered mind to do all its dirty work. Self grasping, the root negativity, can't be in the nature of mind because of the second element of *Selwa*, the '*shunyata* nature' of the mind; and its lieutenant general, self-centered mind, can't be in the nature of mind because it is just a polluted form of Fundamental Positivity. A polluted form of Fundamental Positivity cannot be inherently negative because its underlying base is Fundamental Positivity, itself. Hence, Buddha maintains that there is no inherent negativity; it is only a distorted form of positivity. This will be dealt with in detail in a later chapter.

The conventional fundamental nature of mind establishes negativity as adventitious and removable from the mind. The next question is how negativity can be removed and, more importantly, be removed permanently. For this, the ultimate fundamental nature of mind, which is the *shunyata* of mind, comes into play. The emptiness of mind makes negativity adventitious and removable forever. Having an insight into the *shunyata* nature of the mind will successfully expel negativity from the mind permanently. Since the nature of mind is *shunyata*, empty of self-existence, the root of negativity, self-grasping ignorance, becomes unsustainable. The fact that the mind is *shunyata*, empty of self-existence, shakes the very foundation of negativity. Root negativity and its retinue of negativities feed on clinging to a self-existent 'I' and mine. To fully grasp this, however, some understanding of emptiness is required. This will be covered in a later chapter on the 'profound path.'

To fully grasp *Selwa*, it is essential to establish and understand its two components: the conventional nature (Fundamental Positivity) and the ultimate nature *(shunyata)* of the mind, and how they complement each other in establishing the mind as naturally pure. It is crucial to approach the concept of *shunyata* not merely as a fanciful philosophical notion which leads us nowhere, but rather as an integral part of the fundamental understanding of *Selwa*. By recognizing and exploring the interplay between these elements, we can deepen our comprehension of the mind's inherent purity *(Selwa)*.

The question then is, what is positivity, and how is it the nature of the mind? In other words, why is the mind fundamentally positive? This may be the biggest question we have ever faced. Finding an answer to it is tantamount to discovering the greatest secret. The answer may be so simple that we wonder, 'How did I miss it?'

FUNDAMENTAL POSITIVITY

Are you ready to uncover and behold the greatest treasure within yourself? A treasure that is like water; so simple, yet indispensable to life? Nobody can survive without water, but how often do we appreciate its value? We use water to clean everything, our body, our clothes, vehicles, and home. Similarly, the naturally existing positivity in our mind is indispensable to our temporary and lasting happiness. On its basis we can cleanse all negativity and also reach a perfect level of positivity. Yet we rarely even acknowledge its existence, let alone appreciate it!

If you truly desire to discover your Fundamental Positivity, the journey begins within. Look not outside, to the future or the past, but deep within yourself, in this present moment. Start by directing your attention inward and becoming aware of your physical body, then focus on your breath. As you inhale and exhale, immerse yourself in the entire breathing process—the cool air entering your nostrils, filling your chest, and expanding your abdomen. As you exhale, feel the contraction of your abdomen and the warm air leaving your nostrils. Cultivate a vivid awareness of this intricate dance of breath, appreciating the wonder of your *Rigpa*, the awareness that enables this experience. Appreciate that you are alive; rest are bonuses!

After some time, gently shift your focus from the breath to your mind—specifically, its clarity and knowing. Here, you become aware of awareness itself, much like a mirror reflecting another mirror with no reflection. This is when you touch the fundamental nature of your mind. Take a moment to calmly rest in this awareness. If you find yourself losing it, return to the focus on your breath for a while and then, once again, gently shift back to awareness of awareness, itself—mirror reflecting mirror without reflection.

Over time you will have various experiences. Sometimes awareness seems empty like space; sometimes it is blissful; and sometimes it is simply awareness that just reflects or knows whatever appears before it without conceptualization. Out of these three attributes, emptiness, bliss, and non-conceptual awareness, focus now on that mere awareness. Awareness allows infinite possibilities, from mere knowing, to perceiving, to thinking, projecting, cognizing, feeling, emotionalizing, wishing, and so on. All these manifestations arise from the nature of awareness.

At first, *Rigpa's* luminous function of mere knowing is simply conscious of whatever is present. As a need to penetrate more deeply arises, your awareness can go beyond mere knowing and assume the form of thinking, projecting, anticipating, and cognizing; is my breathing good? Am I doing okay? What could Fundamental Positivity be? As you leave aside mere awareness by thinking and projecting, it leads to a concluding cognition— this is this, that is that, and so on. Then, another type of awareness, a feeling, will be generated as a byproduct of that. Depending upon the feeling that develops, happiness, suffering, or neither of the two, another aspect of awareness in the form of emotion, a desire, or wish will develop. No one can escape having this very fundamental and instinctive wish.

Now, to embark on the search for Fundamental Positivity, let us focus on that final aspect of awareness: the wish. Ask this fundamental wish two simple questions: "What is it that you genuinely wish for?" and "What is it that you do not wish for?" Your spontaneous, authentic, and deeply felt answers will unveil your Fundamental Positivity. It is within these answers that our most precious treasure, Fundamental Positivity, is laid bare—a sanctuary where we can find solace, healing, and unwavering positivity amidst life's chaotic and bewildering circumstances.

Inanimate objects like stones or computers lack the capacity to experience happiness or suffering. However, for sentient beings with feelings, it is impossible not to have a natural wish for happiness and to avoid suffering. This innate desire is an integral part of the mind's natural function, and is inseparable from our consciousness. It is deeply rooted in the fundamental nature of our mind and is naturally positive.

Consequently, positivity naturally resides within the minds of all beings, leaving no room for negativity to be in the natural home of the mind. When we engage in introspection and uncover this fundamental wish, we reveal our greatest secret—*Selwa*, our cherished inner child—Fundamental Positivity. Hold it, accept it, and cherish it like nothing else, because our lasting happiness and abundance of positivity will depend on how well we treat it.

In order to fully unravel this secret, we must contemplate the following: According to Buddha we are living beings because we have a mind with two attributes: awareness and clarity. Awareness provides us the capacity to be aware of things by perceiving, thinking, wishing, feeling, and emotionalizing. There can be positivity or negativity in all of these, and as a result we have both positive and negative feelings and emotions. 'Negative feeling,' means suffering and 'positive feeling' means happiness. When these arise, our innate inclination is to instinctively yearn for happiness and to seek freedom from suffering. This fundamental wish is inherent and instinctive within our minds. As long as the mind exists, feelings will arise, and as long as feelings of happiness and suffering persist, the innate and instinctive aspiration to attain happiness and liberation from suffering will endure. This instinctive wish exists in all sentient beings, and is the conventional nature of Selwa—Fundamental Positivity!

All of us have this fundamental wish because we have feelings of happiness and suffering, not because there is something out there that we like or dislike. These feelings are defined by what our fundamental, uncontaminated awareness instinctively wants or does not want. We have many layers of wishes, most of which are attachments we have accumulated since birth. Wishes for things like a delicious meal, nice clothes, nice weather, a good education, a well-paid job, a beautiful house, a healthy body, long life, are not fundamental wishes. If we peel off all these layers of wishes down to their nucleus, we will reach the wish that is the most fundamental, innocent, natural, and source of all other wishes. It is our innate wish for happiness and to avoid suffering. When we are born, we cry because of this wish. This fundamental wish does not specify happiness as 'my happiness' or 'others' happiness.' Rather, it simply wishes for happiness and not for suffering.

Another reason that we cannot escape this natural wish for happiness and to avoid suffering is the very definition of happiness and suffering. What is happiness and suffering? What defines them? In fact, they are defined by our very fundamental wish! Happiness is what we naturally want and suffering is what we don't. It's simply nature. That's it. This fundamental wish is in the very nature of our mind. It is not something that develops later; we are born with it. Whoever has mind has feeling, and whoever has feeling has this fundamental wish. Nobody from the tiniest insect to enlightened beings can escape this fundamental wish. Though the enlightened beings have this wish in its perfected form. Therefore, I ask you to look deeply within and reflect. Do you sense this fundamental wish?

Another simple, yet greatest, secret is that this fundamental wish is *positive*. How is this wish, which even the most negative person possesses, positive? To answer this clearly, we must first know what is meant by the terms, 'positive' and 'negative.' Buddha gave a very simple and practical answer: anything that is skillful and concordant with this fundamental wish is positive, and anything that is unskillful and in conflict with this fundamental wish is negative. In other words, anything that causes happiness and reduces suffering is positive because it accords with our fundamental wish; and anything that causes suffering

FUNDAMENTAL POSITIVITY

and hinders happiness is negative because it is in contradiction with our fundamental wish. If the very definition of positive and negative is based on this fundamental wish, how can it not be positive?

To categorize these in more detail:

1) Anything that brings about happiness on a temporary basis, but does not bring lasting happiness or cause suffering in the long run is a small positive.
2) Anything that brings about happiness now and in the long run is a big positive.
3) Anything that causes small suffering temporarily, but in the long run brings about happiness, is positive.
4) Anything that causes suffering now but brings neither suffering nor happiness in the long run is a small negative.
5) Anything that causes suffering now and brings about suffering in the long run is a big negative.
6) Anything that causes happiness in you but is neutral for others is a small positive.
7) Anything that brings about happiness in you as well as others is a big positive.
8) Anything that brings about happiness for others but causes temporary suffering in you is still positive because, ultimately, it will bring happiness to you.
9) Anything that causes suffering in you but is neutral for others is a small negative.
10) Anything that causes suffering in you as well as suffering for others is a big negative.

In short, positive and negative are defined by whether they bring about happiness or cause suffering for you or for others. If being positive is about producing happiness and reducing suffering, then our universal fundamental wish is definitely positive because it simply wishes for happiness and the reduction of suffering. Isn't that simple and clear?

Therefore, respectful of every living being, I must say that all people, from the most negative, like Hitler or Stalin, to the most inspiring, like Buddha, Jesus, and Tsongkhapa, all have this naturally existing positivity within them, right from birth. Who could say that the baby Hitler was evil? It is a tragedy that no one had the courage to teach him about Fundamental Positivity and the methods to develop, nourish and enhance it. As a result, his Fundamental Positivity was severely obscured and contaminated, resulting in immense suffering to himself and so many others.

Our fundamental wish desires happiness, without discriminating between *my* happiness and *others'* happiness. It simply wants happiness. Discrimination comes later when negative energy creeps in. The time when negativity begins to emerge is when we first think 'I' and generate a sense of self. The happiness that the fundamental wish concerns itself with is not associated with self or other, or with any fabricated labels such as of nationality, race, social status, and so on. It just knows the naked truth: that happiness is naturally desirable. It is not because of it being American happiness or Tibetan happiness, white happiness, black happiness, high class, or middle-class happiness, human happiness, animal happiness, but because of the mere fact that happiness is simply happiness: desirable and to be cherished. Hence our fundamental wish is definitely positive by nature.

The question arises, why is there so much negativity and suffering when we all have a fundamental wish that is naturally positive? This is because, even though all of us have this naturally existing positivity, it is minuscule. It is a seed, like a baby, naïve and easily manipulated. Therefore, if we want happiness, whether is temporary or lasting, then we must cultivate, nourish, and care for our Fundamental Positivity as our most precious inner child, and not let it be obscured or contaminated.

We have this fundamental wish in the nature of our mind, and it is positive. Ironically, however, we develop negative mental states on the basis of it. This is because we do not know how to nourish and care for our fundamental positivity. Buddha, Tsongkhapa, Jesus and other great beings knew this secret. They nourished and enhanced it to the level of perfection and experienced the highest degree of lasting happiness.

Yet we neglect and obscure it. Based on our fundamental positive wish, we narrow it to wishing for *our own* happiness and *our own* freedom from suffering. We connect happiness and suffering with our sense of self. It is still positive to want happiness without a specific intention to include or exclude others. Where negativity creeps in is when we start to cling to self, and develop attachment on that basis. The attachment to self causes an afflicted wish that desires happiness for ourselves disproportionately, such that our own happiness becomes more important than that of others. Avoiding, lessening and eradicating our own suffering becomes more important than doing the same for others. Happiness and suffering of others lose significance and we become oblivious to it. The negativity becomes even worse when our wish for happiness becomes so afflicted that we seek to attain it at the expense of others;

or to reduce our own suffering even if it causes suffering for others. Alas, at that point our positive fundamental wish, our most precious child, has become obscured and spoiled by negativity. This afflictive wish, known as 'self-centered mind', is a selfish kind of attitude that causes all suffering, fear, and harmful actions.

When we investigate this self-centered attitude, it is not inherently negative; rather, it is an exaggerated and polluted form of our fundamental positive wish. A healthy cell of Fundamental Positivity has mutated into a cancerous cell of selfishness. This, of course, does not mean that our afflicted mind is positive. It is negative because it gives rise to suffering and deprives us of lasting happiness, even if it might sometimes provide us temporary happiness. Since negativity is a polluted form of positivity, it has hints and traces of positivity which is why it can still lead to happiness, but only temporary, superficial happiness. Since it is polluted, it can never lead to genuine happiness; not until we purify it, nourish it, and develop it limitlessly.

It is important to ponder this. As the great master Shantideva (8th C.) says, all negativities — be they actions, feelings, emotions or experiences, both individually and collectively — come from this afflicted, self-centered mind. There is no denying this; it can be verified by our own experience.

Since humankind has existed there have been countless 'discoveries.' Facts are revealed, but later on, many of these 'facts' are disproven or changed. This might leave us wondering what to believe. One thing that will never change, no matter how many scientific and philosophical theories are propounded, is our Fundamental Positivity. It provides us the foundation on which all spiritual practice can be based. It can be the source of infinite positivity. We can comfortably rely upon it with trust. So long as we have feelings, the positive wish for happiness and to avoid suffering will always be there. Nothing can discredit this fact; not scientific experiments nor scriptural authority. It serves as a rock-solid foundation upon which we can build a castle of happiness. Whether it be genuine, lasting happiness, or temporary, superficial happiness, depends entirely upon how we mold Fundamental Positivity. If, in the midst of a challenging life journey, we are seeking solace, peace, healing, dependability and reassurance from our entire spectrum of mind, then look not elsewhere for such a sanctuary than within it. Once you find it, cherish it, hold it dearest, always be aware of it, appreciate it for being naturally positive and protect it by acting in accordance with it. Refrain from doing anything that is not harmony with it. By doing so, you will transform sufferings and experience genuine happiness.

NEGATIVE POTENTIAL

Remember, there is no negativity which exists in the very nature of the mind. When the mind, based on ignorance of the true nature of reality, goes astray from its natural form and temporarily assumes an artificial form, it functions to produce suffering for ourselves and others. This happens when it becomes negative. Every cell in our body is precious for life until it starts to malfunction. Then it causes illness and could even turn into a life-threatening cancer. Similarly, negativity is a temporary aspect that our mind takes on when, as a result of misconceiving the true nature of reality, it goes terribly wrong and causes suffering. This very nature of negativity reveals why it is not in the nature of the mind.

Let's take an example of how self-centered mind, which is negative, comes into being as a result of contaminating our Fundamental Positivity. It is a distorted form of it. Without our positive fundamental wish, we would not develop it. Do inanimate things like stones have a feeling of self-importance? No, because they do not have the Fundamental Positivity that can be polluted in the first place.

NEGATIVE POTENTIAL

The transition from Fundamental Positivity to self-centeredness goes like this: In the natural state, our mind just wants happiness and to avoid suffering. Then it becomes slightly gross by developing a sense of 'I', and then wishing for ourselves to be happy and not to have suffering. At this point it is still positive, but a small positive because it wishes happiness just for ourselves, without explicitly excluding others. That is the point when negativity creeps in and obscures our perception of reality. (This is a crossroads where we can also take another direction, and begin to expand Fundamental Positivity infinitely, as vast as space.) Our sense of self is further reinforced or reified, a self-existent identity to be held onto and grasped at. This pollutes our fundamental wish into a distorted, unfounded, self-centered attitude. It happens so quickly that we cannot grasp what is happening.

This afflictive attachment is further reinforced by various types of ignorance that derive from the basic misconception of ourselves as self-existent:

1) Not knowing that I and all other living beings are equal in having this fundamental positive wish. In other words, not knowing this greatest secret about living beings.
2) Not knowing that not only does '*my*' suffering belong to me, but that the suffering of '*others*' belongs to me as well.
3) Not knowing that not only does my happiness belong to me, but that the happiness of others also belongs to me.
4) Not knowing that the fundamental wish to be happy and not to suffer is a naturally existing positivity of the mind
5) Not knowing that this fundamental wish can be enhanced to a level of perfection

6) Not knowing that the process of enhancing this fundamental wish is a true path that leads to lasting happiness.
7) Not knowing that negativity is not in the actual nature of the mind. It is only adventitious, a temporary 'add-on' that can be 'removed.'
8) Not knowing that negativity can be reduced to zero such that it will never arise again. Not knowing that this can be realized through three deepening levels of insight into the nature of reality: those arising from learning, contemplation, and meditation.

When we look at the mechanism of negativity, we find that the fundamental positive wish is misused by a host of negative mental states grounded in a fundamental misconception of self. This gives rise to attachment to our own happiness which, in turn, mutates into a self-centered mind. This is the mother of all problems, depression, anxiety and so on.

There are many negative mental states: anger, malice, self-centeredness— these are not very difficult to recognize as negative. What is difficult to realize is how our fundamental misconception of self is the root of negativity; and how this misconception gives rise to all other negative minds. The mechanism by which negativity develops can never be established without identifying its root. According to Buddha, all negativity is attributable to a single root cause: a misconception that we and everything around us exist from its own selves independently from consciousness designating it.

The question then arises, does destroying that misconception amount to eradicating all negativity? Is it possible that, even without this root ignorance, there could still be afflictive minds of anger, attachment, malice, jealousy, selfishness, and so on?

It is crucial to pinpoint the root cause of negativity. Otherwise, we will miss the target. The idea of eradicating all negativity will make sense only when we have correctly recognized its root cause and look for a powerful antidote. Eradication of negativity means eliminating all negativity completely, with no possibility of it ever arising again. Of course, this is not a small issue. Most of us have never thought about the possibility of doing this, much less have actually done it. Those who do not particularly concern themselves with this would still do well to develop a conceptual understanding of it, because even a simple conviction that eradication of negativity could be possible gives confidence, a sense of fulfillment and meaning to life. This, in turn, contributes to developing the basic level of lasting happiness. In order to develop a basic level of lasting happiness, the actual eradication of all negativity is not necessary. In order to achieve the highest level of lasting happiness or Buddhahood, however, the eradication of all negativity is a must. Still, a conviction based on valid reasoning that all negativity can be eradicated is crucial to both the basic and highest levels of lasting happiness as it offers a meaningful perspective on life.

Looking further into the mechanism of negativity—first we misconceive 'I' as an independent, intrinsic reality, existing on its own. Existing on its own implies that it exists without depending upon any other factor which is not itself including consciousness designating it. I am not denying the mere existence of 'I;' only the I that is grasped by this misconception. Contrary to how it appears, the I exist interdependently, by designation dependent upon other factors. No phenomenon can withstand analysis that goes beyond mere designation. Therefore, we must be satisfied with an 'I' that is merely designated upon other factors, *others which are not I*. Our 'I' is dependent on many things that are not I: our body, our mind, and other factors. If we are not satisfied with this mode of existence of 'I' and try to find something beyond the mere designation, we find nothing. The 'I' is not findable when we look beyond mere designation because all things on which it is designated are not 'I,' and it is not found anywhere else, either. The fact that the 'I,' when analyzed, is not found, is its lack of independent existence; this is its ultimate nature. In Buddhism it is called Emptiness. I will discuss Emptiness in the chapter called The Profound Path.

Since negativity is adventitious, it can be reduced, bringing our mind to its original, pure state, which is naturally positive. But once we reduce negativity to its basic form, which is positivity, we shouldn't stop there, because our fundamental wish is still very small, naïve and vulnerable, like a little baby. We need to enhance our naturally existing positive wish to attain lasting happiness.

Lasting happiness and positivity are inherently intertwined. In fact, according to Buddhism, Buddhahood, the highest level of lasting happiness, is not possible without enhancing Fundamental Positivity to its perfection and reducing root negativity to zero, never to arise again.

The way of enhancing Fundamental Positivity will be explained in the chapter called The Vast Path.

MEDITATION, PATH OF THE INNER WORLD OF MIND

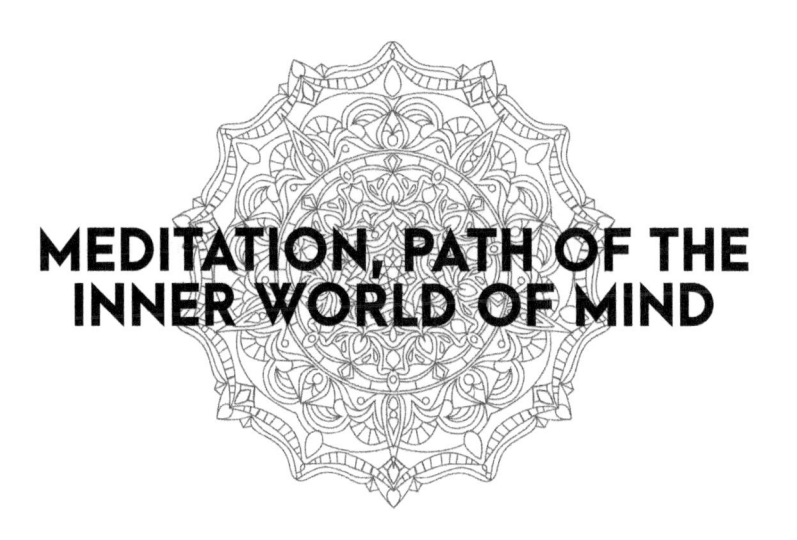

In our pursuit of happiness and dispelling suffering, we exhaust ourselves trying to generate the physical and mental happiness that derives from enjoyment of sense pleasures. Be that as it may, at the same time we would be well advised to take some interest in caring for our mind and nourishing it to develop the lasting happiness that does not, and cannot, arise from enjoyment of sense pleasures. If we do this it is the most skillful way to balance our lives. The best fuel to rejuvenate our mind is lasting happiness. Striking a balance between these two – using some of our energy for temporary happiness but, at the same time, recharging our mind by feeding it the delicious nourishment of lasting happiness– is a truly noble thing. We can induce materially-creatable happiness by acquiring physical things, such as money, a job, a house, etc, but for lasting happiness we need to train and transform our mind.

The most effective way to train and transform our mind is through meditation. In the context of this book, we meditate on three paths; the Foundation Path, the Vast Path, and the Profound Path. To feel comfortable about meditation, and to encourage ourselves to meditate, let us consider the following questions and get an overview of meditation.

WHAT IS MEDITATION? HOW DOES IT WORK?

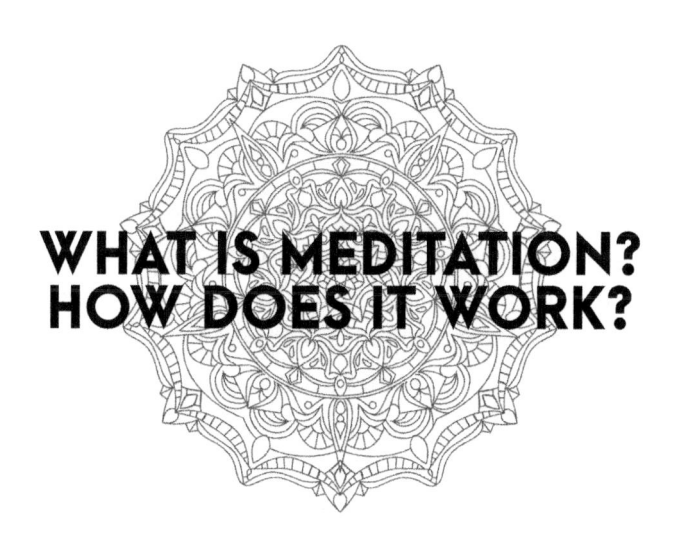

If we come to understand the true meaning of meditation, it will help dispel the stigma that meditation is something mystical, only to be practiced by ascetics; or even worse, weirdos. Or, that it is a passive thing which is impractical for real life. Preconceived notions that they are incapable of meditation is a mental block that many people have. Besides that, we all seem to have a natural laziness when it comes to meditation. If we were given a choice to do thirty-minutes of meditation or dig a hole in the backyard, many of us would prefer the latter. These misconceptions and unfounded tendencies can be dispelled by a correct understanding.

Meditation is a universally practicable method. It is a practical and active method for experiencing happiness that is not generated from objects of the senses. Yes, it may not produce the kind of happiness that depends upon material things. There is no doubt, however, that meditation can help develop happiness, calm, clarity, and contentment that contribute to and enhance enjoyment of even materially-generated happiness. For example, if we are mentally calm and happy, even a cup of coffee tastes far better and is more enjoyable.

Here we need to draw a clear line distinguishing between these two types of happiness and the ways to attain them. Confusion and misunderstanding arise when we lack insight into their true meanings. Dependent happiness, the happiness that depends upon enjoying objects of the senses, must be acquired by obtaining concordant external things; whereas 'non-dependent' happiness— happiness that does not depend upon objects of the senses — is created by the mind itself. Dependent happiness is very limited in the happiness it provides, though easier to acquire. Although it can give both physical and mental happiness, it can do so only up to a certain point; it then becomes stagnant and may even turn into suffering, causing anger, frustration, obsession, anxiety, and sadness. This is where non-dependent happiness must play its role: by not allowing dependent happiness to turn into suffering and afflictions. Non-dependent happiness stops negativity from developing, and provides a basis and way for positivity to grow. This is how we can combine the two happinesses and make our lives meaningful, peaceful, productive, and creative. Can money buy happiness? Some say it can't, others say it can! If we understand the two happinesses we can answer the question once and for all: money may help to experience dependent happiness, but non-dependent happiness cannot be bought. Period!

Since all of us would like to have both dependent and non-dependent happiness, let us not think of meditation as unnecessary, as something to be discarded. If there were another method that could provide non-dependent happiness, hats off to it! Sadly, none has been found so far. We have to try meditation since it seems to be the only reliable solution available! When we are hungry, we don't take a shower instead of going to eat! Similarly, if we want dependent happiness, material happiness, we need to acquire the concordant material things; but if we want happiness that is not dependent upon material things, we shouldn't look outside, but within our own mind. Meditation helps us to look within and explore into the wonders of our inner world. While we naturally look in the right places when it comes to dependent happiness, for non-dependent and lasting happiness we often search in the wrong places.

In a nutshell, temporary happiness can serve as a foundation for developing lasting happiness, but it should not be seen as essential or indispensable for attaining lasting happiness. Otherwise, we risk making lasting happiness dependent on temporary happiness, essentially equating the two. Attempting to make lasting happiness temporary would defeat the very purpose of seeking lasting and genuine happiness.

Meditation is a wonderful tool that can directly affect our mind because we use the mind to train the mind. When someone takes drugs such as opium, LSD, or cocaine, they alter their state of mind through chemical reactions in the brain. This changes the mind through a physical agent. As a result, the effect is not long lasting, and can ultimately be very negative.

Let me explain the idea of meditation through the analogy of a crystal mirror. Mind is like a crystal mirror and its two attributes of awareness and clarity are like a mirror's reflectivity and clarity. Imagine a crystal mirror that is facing a black wall. When you look into the mirror, you will see nothing but black. Suppose someone asked you to clean the surface of the mirror and remove the blackness. Would you go and rub the surface of the mirror with a piece of cloth? You would soon get exhausted by endless cleaning and give up. You would complain that the blackness is in the nature of the mirror!

If you understood that the mirror's blackness was not the nature of the mirror, only a reflection of the black wall, then you would apply a different solution to wipe the blackness from the mirror. Maybe you would move the mirror away from the black wall and place it to face a clear sky, and then a white wall. Bingo! You 'cleaned' the mirror!

Let's apply this metaphor to the meaning. The crystal mirror is like our own mind that we use to meditate, and the black wall is like a negative object or a distorted interpretation of reality that we develop in our daily life. The crystal mirror appearing black when facing the black wall is like our mind obscured with negativity when awareness *(Rigpa)* interacts with negative phenomena. The act of moving the crystal mirror away from the black wall, towards clear space is like first subduing the distorted and negative mind and restoring it to its original, natural state of mere awareness. Then, placing it in front of a white wall is like meditation in which we bring our mind closer to the true nature of reality. The result of facing the white wall, the crystal mirror becoming white, represents our mind becoming more positive as a result of meditation. Rubbing the crystal mirror without the desired result is like trying to bring about enduring positive change in our mind without resorting to meditation.

An interesting thing we can learn from this analogy is the basic mechanism of negativity and its nature. The mirror becomes black as a result of being in front of the black wall. In reality, however, it has not turned black; it just appears to be black. The blackness reflected in the mirror has never been a natural part of the mirror. The luminous nature of the mirror not being in the nature of blackness is like **Selwa** and reflectivity of the mirror is like **Rigpa**. Similarly, in the actual mechanism of negativity, although our mind is naturally and fundamentally clear (*Selwa*), ignorance makes it negative by generating distorted perceptions. These, in turn, produce negative thoughts, emotions, and feelings, leading to a vicious cycle of conflict in our inner world. This further manifests in negative verbal and physical actions. Yet, all this negativity has never been a natural part of our mirror-like mind.

In order to understand the meaning of meditation, let us first establish four important elements:

Subject – the mind that meditates
Object – a phenomenon to meditate upon
Function – what meditation does
Measure of actual meditation– when our mental training becomes actual meditation

Subject

The subject is the mind, the one that meditates. Simply closing our eyes and sitting in a meditative posture without involving the mind does not constitute meditation. We have various aspects of mind at our disposal: mere awareness, thinking mind, cognitive mind, memory, emotion, and feeling. When meditating, we initially rely on awareness, thinking, and cognitive minds because we have these three readily available to us and can direct them easily.

Object

There are two categories of objects: positive and negative. Remember our definitions of negative and positive: anything that brings about happiness is positive and anything that produces suffering is negative. Based on this, positive and negative objects can be understood as follows: Any object, imagined or actual, that induces happiness or has the potency to bring about happiness when the mind perceives it, thinks about it, and moves closer to it, is a positive object. For example, when we perceive, think about, and finally cognize the fact that all of us share the same fundamental wish — to avoid suffering and experience happiness — this induces within us a positive mental transformation of all-embracing compassion. Therefore, the object of contemplation, that all beings equally possess Fundamental Positivity, is a positive object. The basic criteria for being a positive object is that it accords with reality (it actually exists) and has the potency to induce positivity when the mind becomes familiar with it.

Any object that engenders affliction or has the potential to cause suffering when we perceive, think, and familiarize ourselves with it is a negative object. For example, the inability to perceive that all of us have Fundamental Positivity; or thinking that everyone does not equally deserve to be happy; or thinking that we are only responsible for our own suffering; or the thought that only we deserve to be happy. The more we consciously or unconsciously think about such a distorted object, the more self-centered and egotistical we become. As a result, all the negative emotions such as anger, jealousy, and hatred flock to us like honeybees to a flower. Such objects are therefore negative and we do not meditate on them.

Function

When mind meditates, it familiarizes itself with positive objects by perceiving, thinking and cognizing. We do this with as much stability and clarity as we can muster. By meditating, our mind becomes more positive (an emotion) and generates deep, inner, non-dependent happiness (a feeling).

Meditation is therefore a mental exercise that brings our mind closer to a positive object by perceiving, thinking, analyzing, cognizing, feeling, and emotionalizing. As a result, positive transformation takes place and non-dependent happiness expands. Any mental activity which fulfills this function amounts to meditation. Therefore, meditation is a universally applicable method that can bring about positive transformation in our lives.

Two meditation techniques are recommended— analytical meditation and placement meditation. Placement meditation focuses on the whole spectrum of the meditative object, whereas analytical meditation focuses on its details or its constituent parts. Since placement meditation focuses on the general topic, it is easier to use for single-pointed meditation. Analytical meditation, on the other hand, generates clarity because it examines the details of the object. Both methods are crucial.

Let's take the example of one meditation topic: 'All living beings equally possess Fundamental Positivity.' We use placement meditation for this. At first we focus our mind on the topic by thinking, every living being equally possesses Fundamental Positivity. We hold this thought for a while and then follow it up with analytical meditation, examining in detail how all living beings possess Fundamental Positivity. We further meditate on our own experience and the reasons stated above which establish that every living being possesses Fundamental Positivity. When we come to the conclusion that every living being possesses Fundamental Positivity, we simply rest our mind on the meditative object. We alternate between analytical meditation and placement meditation.

This is one set of meditations. We will apply both placement and analytical meditations to each of our topics of meditation. For instance, out of the three paths to lasting happiness, the first we will discuss has several meditative topics and details which will require an equivalent number of placement and analytical meditations. If we use placement meditation alone, we won't have clarity and intensity of mind. Therefore, we should do placement meditation on a meditative topic, followed by analytical meditation on its details. Analyzing the meditative topic in detail generates great clarity and intensity. Analytical meditation will eventually lead us back to placement meditation on our meditative object, with greater clarity and intensity. I will explain later how to assess whether our mental exercise has become true meditation.

With this explanation I hope you have become somewhat familiar with meditation. Now I am going to explain the paths that lead to happiness that cannot be created by material objects of the senses. The word, 'path' here refers to a path of the inner world, which is basically mental training and development. To put it simply, a path is a set of systematic meditations on general topics and their details that we will analyze, cognize, contemplate, and merge with. This is how we 'walk' an inner path.

Measure of Actual Meditation

It is important not only to meditate correctly, but also to know when meditation has become actual meditation. Doing meditation is fairly easy, doing it correctly can be somewhat difficult, and doing it consistently so that it becomes actual meditation is even more difficult. Many do meditation on a daily basis but without knowing whether their meditation is just a mental exercise or true meditation; or at least something leading towards true meditation. Many complain about the ineffectiveness of their meditation, particularly on an emotional level. Doing meditation on a daily basis, they find that it changes their thoughts but not their emotions. I always ask them to learn the measure of actual meditation, and then check whether their own meditation has reached that level. The act of meditating can only yield observable effects on emotion and feelings when it becomes actual meditation.

By way of degree of subtlety, there are three types of objects of meditation: evident, manifest objects such as a table or one's breathing; hidden or subtle objects such as the ultimate nature of phenomena, the mechanism of negativity, and the existence of Fundamental Positivity within us; and an extremely hidden things that are even more subtle that require special mode of analysis in order to understand them. Meditation on evident objects does not require much analysis; single-pointed meditation with clarity and stability is enough. As we meditate repeatedly and reach a point at which our mind is stable and clear and also seems to have penetrated and dissolved into the object, then our meditation has become actual meditation with respect to its manifest and evident object, the table.

As for hidden objects such as how positivity naturally exists within us, we require two wisdoms prior to meditating on them; wisdom derived from listening and learning, and wisdom derived from contemplation. Based on these we are then ready to meditate on hidden objects. It is impossible, at first, to simply place our mind single-pointedly on such an object. Detailed analysis is required in order to place our mind comfortably on the object. Take one hidden object, for example: "How negativity is not the nature of the mind". This is a hidden object because it requires some learning and contemplation prior to meditation. Once we have studied and contemplated sufficiently, we meditate on the topic with analysis and single-pointed focus. As we analyze the meaning, we rely on an internal dialogue that mentally makes use of words to describe the meanings to be understood. As we repeatedly practice this, we reach a point at which we no longer need to rely on the inner dialogue to touch the bare meaning of the topic, to know, directly, how negativity is not the nature of the mind. That is the point at which meditation on a hidden topic becomes actual meditation. Prior to that it was a mental exercise or an 'act' of meditation, but did not fulfill the measure of actual meditation. Actual meditation will have an effect on emotion as well as thought, whereas a less profound practice of meditation may not.

As for the third category, 'extremely hidden things that are even more subtle,' such as subtle karmic cause-and-effect relationship and the mental qualities of fully enlightened beings, we won't delve much into them in this book as they are not highly relevant.

THE ACTUAL WAY TO DEVELOP LASTING HAPPINESS

Remember, we are all explorers of our own inner world, our mind. The path we take is a mental path of meditation, which will gradually lead us to our destination of sublime, lasting happiness. Our mind is the 'walker' and it 'walks' by means of meditation.

First our mind finds the positive reality by means of perception, thinking and valid cognition. These three are processes of learning. At that stage we can transform our thoughts into positive and wholesome thoughts, but not necessarily our feelings and emotions. We might therefore think that analytical meditation is only good for transforming thought; not emotions and feelings. This may be why some scholars of spirituality do not seem to have been transformed by their knowledge!

As beginning meditators, we transform our mind through thought and cognition. As we continue to meditate using the same thinking and cognition, aided by mental stability and clarity, we come closer to positive realities. With continued meditation we reach a point where our mind becomes as if fused or merged with those positive realities. We then no longer need to rely upon mentally reciting the words that describe the meaning; as soon as we think of it, we directly know the meaning, without the necessity of going through a process of inner dialogue. Then we have our first experience of actual meditation, which can affect our feelings and emotions, directly. Until reaching that point, we shouldn't blame meditation for not freeing us from afflictive emotions! We must be patient. Since even acquiring materially-creatable happiness takes time and effort, of course it will take time and effort to attain sublime non-materially-creatable happiness. Be wise and patient!

We have the most important resource: our own mind to walk the path of the inner world. The other thing we need is the positive realities. Finding positive realities means understanding them clearly. Understanding them clearly includes being certain about them, free from doubt. When we doubt, the mind cannot rest stably on its object. When our mind perceives positive realities, it naturally becomes an inner path. Why? When the mind meditates on positive realities it generates positivity and induces inner happiness. These two criteria are similar for all the paths: After perceiving positive realities, then continuously meditating on them in order to engender positive transformation amounts to walking the inner path. The Foundation Path, Vast Path, and Profound Path all involve first understanding positive realities and then meditating on them; which in turn leads to positive mental transformation with genuine happiness as a byproduct.

There are three types of negativities which contaminate Fundamental Positivity; these are dealt with by the three paths. When we identify negativities, we can practice more effectively; it is like knowing the target to be eliminated. The three negativities are: 1) misuse of Fundamental Positivity, 2) contamination of Fundamental Positivity (self-centeredness), and 3) apprehending the self of self-centeredness to be self-existent.

The first of these, misuse of Fundamental Positivity, is addressed by the Foundation Path. When we anticipate or face problems our mind often misuses Fundamental Positivity as justification for reacting with worry, fear, and anxiety. The Foundation Path deals with this and brings equanimity by pacifying mental afflictions and laying the foundation of a calm, peaceful mind. One of the most prevalent and bothersome hindrances to this, for us as individuals and as a society, is worry. Therefore, I will present the Foundation Path as an antidote to worry. Once that is understood the same methods can be used to deal with related afflictions of fear, anxiety, mild depression, sadness and so forth. In my experience the Vast Path has proven to be more effective than the foundation path for relieving depression and fear, while the foundation path is very effective for calming worry.

FOUNDATION PATH

- Mechanism of Worry
- How To Calm Worry

The thrust of all three paths is towards materially-non-creatable happiness. The Foundation Path is a means to attaining the basic level of such happiness. For this to happen worry must be calmed even in the midst of unending daily life problems. Worry is the main factor that arises in our mental continuum that prevents us from remaining happy for prolonged periods of time.

What is worry? Why do we worry so much? Is worry a natural part of our mind? All of us worry in our lives. We know when we're worried, it's an obvious phenomenon. It is mostly associated with future events; mental factors like anger tend to be related to the present. Worry is so common that we may wonder if it is inevitable in the face of life's problems, thus making it more powerful. When we worry the immediate consequence is loss of tranquility. We can't remain calm. Since we are seeking materially-non-creatable happiness, worry must be dealt with.

Some might say that there is a positive element to worry, because when we worry, we do things to solve the problem. This is partially true because worry is a mind's way of saying that something is wrong, go and deal with it. In actuality it is a wisdom understanding that the problem will cause suffering if not solved that pushes us to find a remedy, not worry. Underneath both, it is our fundamental positivity, not worry, that gives us the will to solve the problem. Worry is just a mask that the mind creates to supposedly deal with the problem. Suppose our loved one is undergoing surgery. We might be filled with worry, while the surgeon conducting the procedure will be devoid of much worry, instead relying more on their wisdom and experience.

By default, when we encounter problems, we tend to worry. Worrying makes us feel uneasy, signaling that something isn't right. Worry can have positive aspects when it arises briefly at the outset of an issue, warning us of impending problems. It should then naturally dissolve back, making way for a creative and energetic wisdom to emerge and take its place, which is only possible with a calm mind.

If we wait for worry to subside only after solving a problem and then worry again when another problem arises, repeating this cycle can be a valid approach if you're seeking only temporary happiness. However, if your goal is lasting happiness, this method falls short. Worry will persist, and, in fact, we inadvertently empower and justify its continued existence.

We worry about many different things: job, house, relationships, health, children. It seems as if the main sources of worry are current problems and problems that might arise in the future. If problems were an inevitable cause for worry, then worry could be pacified only if they were solved. Then we could never be free from worry, since there will always be problems in our lives. Fortunately, this is not the case. This will be dealt with in the section below, "Worry as a Mere Mental Creation."

We all want to be happy and not to suffer. Things that cause suffering and deprive us of happiness are designated as problems. Our three basic necessities are shelter, food and health. Being without a home is a major problem because it causes all sorts of suffering. Not having a house and the factors that contribute to that, such as a lack of income, are problems. Whenever we face a problem or anticipate facing one it causes us mental suffering in the form of worry or worse. Sometimes we worry even without apparent problems. This is because of a latent potency for worry that we have built up in the past.

So, the next questions are how and why do we worry? What is the mechanism of worry? We need to explore this; then we can find a way to deal with it.

Mechanism of Worry

When we encounter a problem, whether it is anticipated, projected or real, our mind spontaneously reacts with the emotion of worry. How does this occur? We worry mainly because we feel our Fundamental Positivity, our most precious inner child, is threatened. In order to counteract the threat, our mind deploy dubious defense mechanism which involves misuse and contamination of our Fundamental

Positivity. The foundation path addresses the misuse of Fundamental Positivity, while the Vast path focuses on dealing with the contaminations. Our mind perceives that problems cause us suffering and deprive us of happiness, in direct contradiction with our Fundamental Positivity which wants our happiness and does not want suffering. Our mind resorts to Fundamental Positivity as a means of justification, scapegoating problems as enemy and thereby disguising itself in the form of worry as defensive shield. How is it that our Fundamental Positivity, the most precious asset of our human mind, can be used to generate worry? In actuality, it is not Fundamental Positivity that causes worry, but its misuse. If Fundamental Positivity is misused it causes afflictions like worry, fear, and anxiety; if it is cared for, nurtured, and enhanced, it brings lasting happiness. That is the secret of The Foundation Path.

Let us examine the mechanism of worry in detail. We all possess Fundamental Positivity— a natural wish to avoid suffering and to experience happiness. We consciously or unconsciously assume that problems inherently cause suffering, and our Fundamental Positivity is averse to that. Problems deprive us of the happiness which Fundamental Positivity seeks. Our mind, seemingly justified by Fundamental Positivity, blames the problem for causing the suffering and ruining our happiness, and then deploys worry as a defense shield to protect our most precious inner child, Fundamental Positivity.

If we are about to lose our house, we know it will bring suffering and many complications, contrary to Fundamental Positivity's wish. Hence, we worry at the prospect of losing our house. Considering this, do we worry because of Fundamental Positivity? No, because even enlightened beings have Fundamental Positivity in its perfected version. What, then, causes our worry? Our mind takes a self-defeating approach towards problems by misusing Fundamental Positivity. We create a mental link that connects problems with worry by misusing Fundamental Positivity. We do not have quite the same reaction to other people's problems because our mind does not instinctively make this link; we do not have a direct mental link to their problems.

The link between problems and worry is an instinctive feeling to blame the problem; "This problem is threatening my inner child so I ought to worry!" The link is actually created by our mind as a defensive response, using Fundamental Positivity as justification. "Our mind is saying, 'Oh no, this is a problem! Since I don't want suffering (Fundamental Positivity) and this problem will cause it, I should worry!' Since I truly want happiness (Fundamental Positivity) and this problem will hinder me from attaining it, I should worry." Our mind, based on Fundamental Positivity, blames the problem in order to create the link: "I ought to worry." If one understands this link correctly both in theory and experience, it will become easy to undo it.

How To Calm Worry

- Returning Home, the Fundamental Nature of Mind
- Performing a Reality Check on Problems
- Turning Off the Problem-Worry Link

Returning Home, the Fundamental Nature of Mind

Any inner exploration has to start from the fundamental nature of mind. The fundamental nature of mind is our home. Most of us have been like an explorer of the outer world, spending most of our time away from home. Now is the time for us to return home and become an inner explorer.

When the mind is consumed by worry it forgets its own nature and identifies with worry. The same goes for fear, sadness, anxiety, and repetitive thought. The way to 'undo' these is to return to our natural home, mind's fundamental nature— clarity and awareness. Mindfulness is the key, the easiest way to open the door to our inner home.

When we worry, the mind is fully submerged in worry, wholly occupied by it. Let's use a part of our mind to observe the mind of worry, and acknowledge its presence. If it is difficult, we can start by observing our breathing and then gradually turn our attention to the worry. A part of our mind previously fused with worry, detaches and observes the worry. The worry will lose some of its intensity because now only a part of the mind remains in the form of worry, while another part returns to its natural form, mere awareness. As we observe, the wave of worry will subside and gradually dissolve back into the great ocean of mind. What remains now is mere awareness and clarity. We have touched the true nature of our mind. We hold on to it as long as we can. Focus on this mere awareness which is clear, pacified of all concepts and afflictions.

As we hold onto this awareness with mindfulness, a mental bliss will arise; this is materially-non-creatable happiness. The mind is meditating on itself. We are aware of the true nature of our mind, mere awareness, characterized by clarity, calm, and bliss. This bliss cannot be produced by any material object. It can only be attained by returning to our inner home. After remaining in mere awareness with intensity and clarity for a while, we can initiate an analytical process to investigate in detail.

Performing a Reality Check on Problems

- Are problems the source of suffering?
- Is worry just a mental construct?
- Developing new perspective on problems

Are Problems the Source of Suffering?

We have seen how our mind misuses Fundamental Positivity to create the, 'I-ought-to-worry' link as a defense mechanism against problems, blaming them for causing us suffering and destroying our happiness. This link has two elements we will need to deal with: our perception of problems and our misuse of Fundamental Positivity to justify worry.

Shantideva said there can be two kinds of problems; one that has a solution and one that doesn't. With respect to the first, since it has a solution, we needn't worry and our approach can be one of energetic wisdom. As for the other, when a problem has no solution, it does no good to worry about it.

How do we instinctively define problems? They are what give us suffering and take away our happiness. Let us examine this perception of problems. Do problems cause suffering and deprive us of happiness? If so, do they cause physical suffering or mental suffering or both?

Many problems have a solution and are fixable. On the other hand, if they are not solved, they may lead to physical suffering. If the problem such as losing a job is not dealt with it may lead to another problem: not being able to pay the mortgage, eventually leading to homelessness. Being forced to live on the street is conducive to tremendous physical suffering, freezing cold in the winter, scorching heat in the summer, illness and so on. It is obvious that problems cause physical suffering if they are not solved. Problems from their side may or may not create physical suffering; they are neutral. If they are solved it will bring happiness and satisfaction; and if not dealt with properly, they may likely cause physical suffering.

Since problems do play a role in producing physical suffering, particularly when they are not solved, they can't be completely absolved of the accusation of being producers of suffering. Now the next question is whether they play any role in producing mental sufferings including worry or not?

Is Worry Just a Mental Construct?

The next question, however, is even more critical for us as seekers of materially-non-creatable happiness, because mental sufferings and materially-non-creatable happiness are mutually exclusive; whereas problems and physical sufferings *can* in fact coexist with materially-non-creatable happiness. Must problems inevitably cause mental suffering? Must they necessarily cause worry to arise?

As a seeker of lasting happiness, we can't afford to wait until all problems are solved for worry to permanently subside. Problems are a part of life and they won't end until life is over. What we can do now is sever the problem-worry link; we can be free from worry even in the midst of daily life's problems. Even though it seems like problems have complete power to induce worry, worry is not caused by problems. Why?

If problems were responsible for causing worry on its own, it should be the case that whenever there is a problem there is worry; and whenever there is no problem there is no worry. This doesn't accord with reality. When I was in first year Prajnaparamita class, I dreaded it and constantly worried. There was a rumor that I had failed the recitation test. Recitation by memory is one of the three major examinations, the other two being debate and a written test. We had to pass all three in order to go to the next level. The rumor had some credibility because I was bad at memorizing texts. I didn't dare attend morning class that day the results were announced because I was afraid of being embarrassed. After prayers, when my friends returned, I was ready to face the dreaded news. None of my friends said anything to me. When I asked about my result, they said I had passed the test, though just barely. As soon as I heard this, the worry that had been nagging me ever since I first heard the rumor evaporated. I had been worrying over a non-existent problem. The worry was a creation of my own mind! It couldn't have come from the problem because there was no problem. This experience convinced me that worry can arise without having an actual problem, and vice-versa. Sometimes there are problems that we don't worry about, either because we are blissfully ignorant of them, or because we modify our attitude towards them.

If somebody loses a hundred thousand dollars they are bound to worry. Losing such an amount is a big problem. Suppose a friend called and said the money was found, even though that wasn't true. The unfortunate person would be relieved until he found out it was a prank. During the intervening period, even though the actual problem was still there, he wouldn't worry. If the problem on its own had the power to cause worry, he should still worry even when he was told that the money was found. Why? Because the actual problem was still there.

These real-life experiences clearly demonstrate that worry is not entailed by problems. It does not follow the problem; it follows the mind. If the mind says there is a problem, worry will arise even when there is no problem. Even when there is a problem, if the mind says it is not a problem, worry won't arise. This shows that worry is not produced by problems, but by the manner in which the mind perceives the problem. Hence, it is just a mental creation. Once we accept that worry is our mind's own creation, our mind takes some responsibility for it, rather than just blaming it on the problem alone. Mind, in its disguise as 'worrier,' has been unmasked! When mind-disguised-as-worry is exposed, it has no choice but to be embarrassed and dissolve back into the mind's nature. Understanding and internalizing that worry is just a mental creation, and not an inevitability of a problem, is the most powerful method to undo the link between problems and worry. Below is a brief inner journey we may embark upon to explore the justice system within our inner world.

In the court of the inner world the verdict has been pronounced: external problems are innocent of causing worry, even though they may cause physical suffering when not dealt with properly. The court has exonerated external problems for causing mental suffering; instead, our mind has been found responsible. This verdict has created havoc and shaken the very foundation of our inner justice system! The prosecutor, our mind-disguised-as-worry, was very strong and confident prior to the verdict. Now it is weakened and been left no choice but to resign. This is like a corrupt prosecutor bringing a misdemeanor charge against an innocent suspect! At the beginning of proceedings the prosecutor was well dressed, had a domineering presence, and spoke loudly. As the case progressed, however, irrefutable evidence emerged pointing the needle of guilt at the prosecutor, himself. Imagine how he would lose credibility, be forced to resign!

When we realize that worry is a creation of our own mind, based on misusing our Fundamental Positivity, we realize that external problems are not guilty of the accusations leveled against them; rather, our mind-disguised-as-worry is the guilty party. When this happens our mind-disguised-as-worry has no choice but to gradually withdraw. It induces within us a confidence that worry can be calmed without necessarily having to solve the problem. This is great news because we don't need to wait until all problems are solved to calm worry permanently.

In the midst of problems seen as challenges, worry can be calmed and energetic wisdom generated in its place. If we realize that worry is a mental construct that can dissolve back into our mind even without solving the problem, it paves the way to shake loose the strong grip that worry has on us.

Developing a New Perspective on Problems

Whenever we encounter problems, especially those that have solutions, we should develop enthusiastic wisdom knowing that they are actually opportunities for us to investigate and untangle them, and to find experiences of happiness lying beneath their surface. Instead of focusing on them as causes of suffering, view them as opportunities that could unravel into varieties of happiness. As we strategize to solve them, we may encounter new happinesses, by surprise!

When I first came to America, I stayed at a friend's house for some months then moved out to settle into a small studio apartment. Within a month I found a notice to vacate pasted on my door. Initially I was worried and angry (the landlord had assured me of at least a year of residency). But, instead of getting bogged down with crippling worry and anxiety, I treated the problem as an opportunity for new happiness. That lightened the heaviness in my mind. As I moved on to solving the problem, the first happiness I discovered was driving a newly released Fiat 500, red edition, which I had rented in order to impress new landlords! I got to see many different neighborhoods and met many nice people. Some of them invited me into their house and we chatted, though not so much about the possibility of renting as about my background as a Tibetan and its fascinating culture. I also received lots of appreciation and curious inquiries about the new Fiat 500, gleefully going along with their assumption that I owned it!

Turning Off the Problem-Worry Link

- Ridiculing the 'default' mindset that uses Fundamental Positivity to justify worry
- Creation of mental tranquility based on Fundamental Positivity is fully justified

Ridiculing the 'default' mindset that uses Fundamental Positivity to justify worry

There is nothing more worthy of ridicule than our default mindset which worries when encountering problems and then justifies it on the basis of Fundamental Positivity. We deploy worry as a defense mechanism towards any enemy that threatens our precious inner child, our Fundamental Positivity; but that defensive strategy ends up threatening what it is supposed to defend! The worry causes more suffering and deprives us of happiness, in direct contradiction to Fundamental Positivity which innately wants happiness and not suffering. Worry is a zillion percent unjustified for its continued existence! Mind misuses Fundamental Positivity to create the 'ought-to-worry' link. We will use the very same Fundamental Positivity to create the link 'worry-ought-to-be-dissolved into tranquility' thereby undoing the previous link. This is another great secret revealed.

Creation of mental tranquility based on Fundamental Positivity is fully justified

When faced with problems, we ought not worry simply because we do not wish to suffer. Since we want happiness, worry ought to be dissolved back into the blissful nature of mind, allowing us to cultivate energetic wisdom that can solve the problem. In this way we use Fundamental Positivity— our wish to have happiness and be free of suffering— as the ground for calming worry. In the process we can cut off the problem-worry link with an ought-to-be-calm link that is justified by Fundamental Positivity. In summary, we should solve the problems by utilizing the Fundamental Positivity, rather than misusing. It's that simple.

In the practice of the Foundation Path, we realize, understand, and feel our Fundamental Positivity, and use it to defuse worry to the level of equanimity. Some might think that without worry we become indifferent to problems and don't care about solving them. This is an unfounded concern because we are giving up worry based on the very fact that we want happiness and don't want suffering. The same reason will apply to the problems. Since we do not wish suffering, and want happiness, we will not ignore problems. Since happiness lies beneath problems, and is revealed when they are solved, we won't be indifferent. Our Fundamental Positivity will motivate us to approach the problem with a calm, strong mind. Worry can never be calmed by simply ignoring the problem. Doing nothing and just having wishful thinking doesn't accord with Fundamental Positivity. Remember that not being in alignment with Fundamental Positivity brings unhappiness, and that being concordant with it brings happiness.

To this point we have learned and contemplated some positive realities pertaining to the Foundation Path: that worry is a misuse of Fundamental Positivity; that the problem-worry link is severable, and so on. We have gained valid cognition of these positive realities. Since worry is an emotion, however, just having positive thoughts can't calm it. We need to deepen our understanding through meditation as it connects our positive thoughts to the entire spectrum of our mind, and brings about changes on an emotional level.

The link in our mind between problems and worry forms right from birth. It is deeply rooted and has become automatic and spontaneous. As soon as we begin to feel, Fundamental Positivity is there; yet, when we encounter problems, the ought-to-worry link is activated as a defense mechanism. Anxiety, fear, and sadness also shoot through this link at the slightest provocation, real or imagined.

To connect our valid thought with emotion and to penetrate and dissolve this deeply seated link, we transform valid thought into meditation. We cannot stop at valid positive thought, because valid thought can only transform thoughts. Worry is an emotion so valid thought alone cannot alter it. To transform the mind at the deeper level of feelings and emotion we need meditation.

Meditation is a deepening of valid thought. Once we have met these positive realities, we go deeper to penetrate them completely. It is like developing a deep bond with a friend. When we contemplate these realities repeatedly there comes a time when our mind merges with them; such meditation transforms not only our thoughts but our feelings and emotions as well.

Here is how we do it. When a worry arises, first just look at it without analysis and let it dissolve into your mind's true nature, mere awareness. The worry fades and bare awareness becomes more prominent. When this occurs, simply hold that awareness because you have reached the fundamental nature of your mind. Be with it: aware of mere awareness. Mind is meditating on mind. Remain in this state until it induces a deep sense of peace within you. Within this state of awareness, calm and clear, meditate by generating valid thought using the new narrative: "Worry ought to be dissolved into the blissful nature of mind because I don't want suffering and want happiness." As you think about this meaning, rely on mentally reciting the words expressing it. Then think about how worry works: that problems may be responsible for physical suffering if not solved, but they are not responsible for creating worry, because worry is a mental construct. Contemplate how worrying based on Fundamental Positivity is ridiculous; and how worry ought to be dissolved into the tranquil nature of mind; and that, within that tranquility, engendering energetic wisdom to solve problems is something noble, truly justified by our Fundamental Positivity.

While we ridicule worry, we shouldn't be too harshly critical of it, because worry can be an indicator of impending problems. Hence, we can tolerate worry's initial appearance, but not its continued existence, and we should make way for creative wisdom to further deal with problems. In this, we are being diplomatic with our worry because we appreciate its intention to protect the inner child, our Fundamental Positivity. This way of dealing with worry makes it easier to dissolve back into our mind.

The Foundation Path Meditation

Sitting comfortably, with your back upright, relax your body. Feel your body: your feet and legs... your bottom on your seat...your waist, torso, arms, neck, head; slowly go through your whole body, noting and relaxing any tension you find.

Now bring your attention to your breath; all the sensations of breathing. Cool air enters your nostrils, filling your abdomen and chest. Air leaves your nostrils as your abdomen contracts and chest falls. Be aware of the whole process, looking inwards, this very moment. Relax any attachment to the past or future.

After a while, gently shift focus from breathing to awareness, itself. Let your mind look at mind, the observer that is aware of everything. This is the fundamental nature of our being. If something like a worry crosses your mind, look at it nakedly, without following it. It dissolves, like a wave subsiding into the ocean. When it subsides, rest in that calm awareness, without thought.

This is the nature of our innermost being, the nature of our mind prior to thinking, feeling, emotionalizing. Let's become familiar with our own mind, unaltered, just as it is! We are returning from our long journey exploring the external world to really look within. We have begun our journey home. It is a good home. It is our fundamental nature. Even though the pull of worry and other afflictive emotions is strong, by not identifying with them we can watch them subside like waves into the ocean. In the midst of the storm of afflictive emotions, without believing our identity is found in them, we come home to our present Fundamental Positivity; our simple wish for peace, happiness, and freedom from suffering. Having rested our mind in this non-analytical meditative state for a while, we are ready to start the actual meditation: going through the details of our investigation. Meditate by analyzing:

I worry when I encounter problems or anticipate them. (If you have no nagging problem then think about general problems; otherwise focus on the specific problem that you are worrying about by first acknowledging its presence). Oh, I am in a state of worry, and it seems like worry arises whenever there is a problem. It also seems like worry can only be calmed by solving the problem. Problems appear to be the main culprit. My mind, taking the role of a prosecutor, arises in the form of worry, claiming authority using Fundamental Positivity to justify its existence. Here, we first say 'thank you' to worry for being so concerned and caring about our inner child, Fundamental Positivity, and giving us a heads-up about problems. Addressing worry, say, 'We appreciate your initial appearance but your continued existence is no longer needed for the reasons to follow.

The problem is charged with being in "direct contradiction to Fundamental Positivity" since it allegedly causes suffering and deprives us of the happiness which Fundamental Positivity naturally wants. But the court of reality has now found that the charges brought against problems don't hold up. Problems do cause physical suffering if not solved, but not mental suffering. Problems may deprive us of physical happiness, but they do not have to affect our mental happiness.

The prosecutor attacks again, saying that problems do cause mental suffering because whenever we encounter problems we suffer with worry, anxiety, fear or sadness. The court of reality strikes back, saying that problems themselves do not cause mental suffering; rather, mental suffering is caused by the way we perceive the problem. Problems are thus absolved of 90% of the charges leveled against them; they are not responsible for suffering. Instead of being thieves of happiness they are just challenges waiting to be surmounted, revealing hidden satisfaction and happiness within.

Since problems are not the culprits, then what is? The justice system finds that the prosecuting worrying mind is responsible. Mind-disguised-as-worry loses its credibility and becomes embarrassed, on the verge of withdrawing into its source. Now the court of reality gives its final verdict. It sends shockwaves through the justice system, and puts the final nail in the prosecutor's coffin! The court finds that the charge of 'being in direct contradiction to Fundamental Positivity' that was leveled against problems falls back on the prosecuting worrying mind, itself! Mind-disguised-as-worry is in direct contradiction to Fundamental Positivity because worry not only causes suffering; it is, itself, of a nature of suffering. And worry not only deprives us of superficial happiness; it deprives us of genuine happiness as well. Therefore, contemplate, 'To protect and nurture Fundamental Positivity, my precious inner child, let worry dissolve! Let calm, energetic, creative wisdom *arise on its behalf, to properly deal with challenging problems and uncover happiness lying beneath!'*

Repeat these last sentences three times. *(As you will continue to practice this meditation daily, there will come a time in the future when your meditation won't require you to repeat those sentences. You will be able to touch the meaning directly without depending on name image. At that point, I guarantee that your worries will have calmed.)*

Measure of Realization of the Foundation Path

Meditating as above on a daily basis, we eventually reach a point where we can directly touch the meaning of the positive realities pertaining to the foundation path; we no longer need to mentally recite the words, sentences, and paragraphs that give the meaning in detail. When this occurs, we have realized the foundation path, and our meditation will have the effect of calming worry instantly.

THE VAST PATH

How to Enhance Fundamental Positivity

In the Foundation Path, we realize, acknowledge, and meditate on the existence of Fundamental Positivity, and utilize it to dissolve worry and other afflictions. This counters the first level of negativity—our default mindset which misuses Fundamental Positivity to justify worry and other afflictions.

The second level of negativity is a contaminated form of Fundamental Positivity that wishes happiness and avoidance of suffering primarily for ourselves. In order to counteract this, we practice the Vast Path.

The Vast Path can be summarized in two: uncovering multiple layers of contamination to reach Fundamental Positivity; and, once found, nourishing and enhancing Fundamental Positivity limitlessly.

Although we have Fundamental Positivity we still suffer. This is because our Fundamental Positivity is small and contaminated by negativity. We need to nourish it and let our Fundamental Positivity expand. In this section will be explained positive realities that we can meditate on in order to nourish our precious Fundamental Positivity. This will automatically induce materially-non-creatable happiness. At the same time, it remedies the second level of negativity.

Finding *Selwa* (Fundamental Positivity)

If you aspire to cultivate a wish-fulfilling tree in your backyard, acquiring its seed is the initial requirement. Only then can you proceed to plant it and provide essential care like fertilizer, water, and sunlight. Similarly, when it comes to enhancing Fundamental Positivity, it is crucial to first discover it within ourselves and then nourish it by sharing it equitably with all living beings. Uncovering Fundamental Positivity is a relatively straightforward undertaking; we delve deeply into ourselves to connect with our deepest aspirations. That's all that is needed to begin this transformative journey.

If we are coming from the Foundation Path, in which we have pacified worry and other afflictions like anxiety, sadness, and fear by relying on Fundamental Positivity, then no other method is needed to find *Selwa*. We just continue to enhance it from there. However, if you are coming directly to practice of the Vast Path, then search for *Selwa* systematically as follows. Again, explore your inner world, probing as you encounter diverse aspects of mind like thoughts, feelings, and emotions. Going deeper, touch the core nucleus of your mind – *Rigpa* and *Selwa*. We find that awareness can assume various aspects: perceiving, thinking, wishing, feeling, emotionalizing, and so on. Out of these various aspects, feelings can be of three kinds; pleasant, unpleasant, or neutral. Based on pleasant and unpleasant feelings, wishes will arise. With further introspection we find in these wishes our Fundamental Positivity; simply wanting happiness and not suffering. If we look carefully at this naturally existing wish, we will understand that it is positive in nature because wishing for happiness and wishing to be free from suffering is positive. Once we understand and are convinced without doubt that this fundamental wish is positive, we have uncovered *Selwa*, our precious inner child.

Our fundamental positive wish is like a young prince who is innocent, vulnerable, and easy to manipulate, but has the potential to become king. Once we have found and recognized Fundamental Positivity, our next step is to nourish it, to expand and enhance it, so it may become the glorious king, Great Nirvana.

Actual Method to Enhance Fundamental Positivity

Once we have found our precious inner child, nourishing and enhancing it is quite simple and easy. The fundamental wish that desires happiness and a cessation of suffering is ever-present within us, mostly in a latent, but occasionally in a manifest form. Whenever it arises, the first moment is pure and uncontaminated. After that, it easily becomes contaminated and covered by egotistical mind that gives rise to layers of afflictive emotions like attachment, anger, fear, and jealousy. In the Vast Path, the point at which we intervene is the initial moment when the fundamental positive wish has just arisen naturally, or else we wake it from its dormant form simply by wishing for happiness and not suffering. Once the wish for happiness and not suffering is manifest, we can 'kick-start' our process of enhancing Fundamental Positivity. When it first manifests, signs that this wish is Fundamental Positivity are the fact that it is not particularly associated with ourselves or others; and that it feels very natural and spontaneous, an integral part of ourselves.

When we intentionally wish for happiness and not suffering, artificially generated Fundamental Positivity will wake up authentic Fundamental Positivity, and merge immediately with it. What we have done is to wake it from a subconscious level to a conscious level; we then use it to meditate. In this way we are 'in sync' with Fundamental Positivity. We touch the very core nucleus of our mind. All mental transformation begins from this point.

Having found Fundamental Positivity, we nourish it to its full blossom of sublime materially-non-creatable happiness. Without enhancing Fundamental Positivity, we cannot develop materially-non-creatable happiness; this is because positivity is the cause of happiness. If we have the seed of a wish-fulfilling tree wrapped up in a box, nothing will happen unless it is unwrapped, planted, given sunlight, water, and fertilizer, and a caring gardener to look after it!

When we begin the process of enhancing Fundamental Positivity, we need a seed that we can nurture. By great good fortune, Fundamental Positivity is the seed and we all naturally possess it. We need to wake it from its latent state and bring it to a conscious, manifest level. This is not as difficult as it might seem. All we have to do is consciously wish for happiness and to avoid suffering. Bingo! Fundamental Positivity is generated within us. At this stage just be aware of it and careful not to contaminate it with egotism. Also be aware that it is positive by nature.

Again, Fundamental Positivity is simply wishing happiness and not wanting suffering. It is not exclusive to ourselves nor does it exclude others. It is natural, spontaneous, within all of us. We don't need to acquire it. Just be aware of it. Being aware of it means finding it. We then strengthen it, starting with ourselves. Here, we can include ourselves without contamination. A way to avoid contamination is to enhance our Fundamental Positivity by increasing its scope and spreading its two wings—wishing happiness on the right and not wishing suffering on the left– to all other beings one by one, using the Fundamental Positivity of others as the ground.

We start by enhancing Fundamental Positivity beginning with ourselves, by generating a sense of ourselves or 'I' associated with Fundamental Positivity. It goes like this: May I be happy and free from suffering since I have Fundamental Positivity.

Next we generate the same wish for our loved ones, starting with our parents, grandparents, spouse, children, and friends. Use Fundamental Positivity as the basis, not other reasons such as, because they are family. Next we include our friends, neighbors and other people we've met. Gradually we expand it to include people from neighboring cities and then the entire country and the world. When we do this meditation, it is good to include as many people as we know or can recognize because it makes our meditation clearer, more focused and intense.

The way to enhance Fundamental Positivity is to increase its scope as much as possible. At this point our Fundamental Positivity has expanded to all people of earth. The wings of Fundamental Positivity can soar far and wide, encompassing all living beings throughout space. After human beings, we can begin including animals, even insects. Finally, we can include every sentient being in the universe. The concept, 'think globally and act locally,' is useful in this context. When it comes to enhancing Fundamental Positivity, the sky is the limit. Since it is done at a mental level, why put a limit on it? Embrace the vastness of living existence, boundless like space. Be grateful for all sentient beings, as they enable the limitless expansion of your Fundamental Positivity. When it comes to enacting and embodying Fundamental Positivity, do that locally by engaging in physical and verbal actions to benefit those with whom one has contact. Even when we are unable to provide physical or material benefit to others in a given moment, we can still extend the wings of our Fundamental Positivity by wishing them the best and refraining from causing them harm. Refraining from causing harm aligns with the left wing of Fundamental Positivity, which is the aspiration to be free from suffering.

We include all sentient beings under the wings of our Fundamental Positivity simply because all beings have Fundamental Positivity. How do we define 'sentient being?' Are there sentient beings on other planets? We may not have a definitive answer to the latter question, but the definition of a sentient being is 'having Fundamental Positivity;' that is the sole criterion. We can include any being, even bacteria, if they meet that criterion. Wherever there are sentient beings, they desire happiness and wish to be free from suffering, so can we expand our Fundamental Positivity limitlessly by including their wish for happiness and freedom from suffering within our own. Here, we equate sufferings and happiness of ourselves and others as one. We grow the seed of our own Fundamental Positivity in the ground of theirs. The defining characteristic of a Buddha is someone who has perfected and fully expanded their Fundamental Positivity.

While the Foundation Path is an effective method for alleviating mental afflictions such as anxiety, sadness, and depression, the Vast Path has even greater potency in this regard. This is primarily due to its ability to directly address the root cause of all mental afflictions—the self-centered mind, which tends to excessively prioritize our own suffering and happiness. Worry, anger, anxiety, sadness, jealousy, fear and many other afflictions arise as a result of Fundamental Positivity being contaminated by self-centered mind. By specifically targeting this aspect, the Vast Path offers a more profound and comprehensive approach to dissolving worry and alleviating mental disturbances. This is another great secret revealed here. Cherish it! Below is a summary of how to utilize the Vast Path to pacify worry and other afflictions.

When you are in a state of mental suffering, be it worry, fear, anxiety, mild depression, one thing is automatic: you instinctively wish to be free from that state. This is due to the fact that Fundamental Positivity already exists within you. Actually, Fundamental Positivity was generated long ago, and by the time worry arises, it has already been contaminated; otherwise, worry and other mental sufferings would not arise. The most skillful way to purify Fundamental Positivity is to spread its wings to encompass all sentient beings. Cultivate a wish that all other sentient beings, along with yourself, be freed from worry, anxiety, fear, depression, and so on. Be gentle and compassionate with yourself by gradually including the sufferings of others under the left wing of your own Fundamental Positivity. Once Fundamental Positivity is purified, brought to its innate state, and enhanced, worries and other afflictions will dissolve automatically into the mind's nature. This method is also helpful in relieving worry and other afflictions that don't seem to have a tangible reason.

In 2005 a group of seven monks from Gaden Shartse monastery including myself traveled to Houston, Texas on a religious tour to create a Green Tara sand mandala. While some monks were assigned to work on the mandala at the museum, a senior monk named Khentrul Rinpoche Tenzin and I were invited by a Vietnamese family to conduct a ritual at their home.

Upon arrival, the mother of the family informed us that their daughter was believed to be possessed by a spirit. The daughter, with long hair covering her face, sat facing us as we prepared to cast off the presumed spirit. To do this, Khentrul Rinpoche chose the Yamantaka ritual, a Buddhist tantric practice.

During the ritual I suddenly experienced intense fear and felt as though an electric current was passing through my brain and body. Overwhelmed, I abruptly stood up, surprising Khentrul Rinpoche and the others, and left the house. Seeking solace, I found myself sitting under a tree in the garden, reminiscent of Buddha's enlightenment.

In the grip of fear, I turned to my practice of nurturing Fundamental positivity. Deep breathing and reflection helped me to acknowledge and be conscious of my fear, as well as my spontaneous wish to be free from it (Fundamental positivity. Remember, wishing to be free from suffering is like the left wing of fundamental positivity.) Then I empathized and thought, 'There must be so many people all over the world going through this same kind of suffering. Since I am already experiencing it, spontaneously wishing to be free from it, why not be more expansive and inclusive by merging the mental suffering of all people on earth with mine and wishing us all to be free of it? As soon as I opened up my fundamental positivity and spread its wings to include others, my fear subsided and I went back to the house. Khentrul Rinpoche inquired about my sudden departure, to which I admitted experiencing intense fear. His reassuring words provided much needed comfort and encouraged me not to succumb to paranoia.

Vast Path Guided Meditation

Sitting upright, relax and feel the presence of your body. Be aware of your breathing. After some time, gently shift your focus from breathing to awareness, itself; calm, clear, and alert.

Present within your bare awareness is an innate wish for happiness and freedom from suffering. This is natural and fundamentally positive, an essential goodness within you. Let's enhance it now by acknowledging it. Allow yourself to wish for happiness! To wish for no suffering! Hold it for a few seconds. Cherish this essential goodness as your greatest treasure.

Now let's begin to spread the wings of Fundamental Positivity, expanding it. First, consciously include yourself. 'May I be happy and free of suffering!' Then, include those dearest to you, your parents, your children, your friends, and so on. Use the words to contemplate and feel the emotion:

May I be happy and free of suffering because I care about my Fundamental Positivity. May I have temporary happiness as well as lasting happiness.

May my children be happy and free of suffering because they have Fundamental Positivity. May they have temporary happiness (of such and such...fill in the details and specifics as you want) and lasting happiness.

May my parents be happy and free of suffering. May they have temporary happiness (fill in details and specifics) and lasting happiness.

May my friend... (say their name) ... be happy and free of suffering. May they have temporary happiness (fill in details) and as well as lasting happiness

May the old lady with the blue cardigan I met today at the supermarket be happy and free from suffering. May she have temporary happiness and lasting happiness

May my co-worker who is not so fond of me be happy and

free from suffering. May they have temporary happiness (fill in details) and lasting happiness because they too have Fundamental Positivity.

Clearly picture people who elicit strong emotions in you and then extend those same emotions to everyone you know or have met remembering their situation is the same. They have the same Fundamental Positivity, wishing for happiness and for freedom from suffering. Feel what they feel, put yourself in their shoes. Starting with close ones, gradually include strangers, then enemies, and finally expand to include all beings throughout space, without losing the intensity of emotion of a personal connection. When it comes to enhancing Fundamental Positivity, never limit yourself; let it be as infinite as sentient beings throughout space. But don't jump to that through over-generalizing; build up to it gradually by focusing in succession on individual and specific beings, maintaining the intensity of the feeling.

Visual Guided Meditation on How to Enhance Your Fundamental Positivity

To begin, familiarize yourself with a visual representation of Fundamental Positivity symbolized by the syllable OM. The script used here is Sanskrit Wartu script to which I've added two wings to facilitate the visualization used in the meditation (fig. 2). The left wing (on the right as you look at the syllable from the front) represents the wish to be free from suffering and the right wing represents the wish for happiness.

TIBETAN BOOK OF HAPPINESS

RIGHT WING: WISH TO BE HAPPY

FUNDAMENTAL POSITIVITY

LEFT WING: WISH TO BE FREE FROM SUFFERING

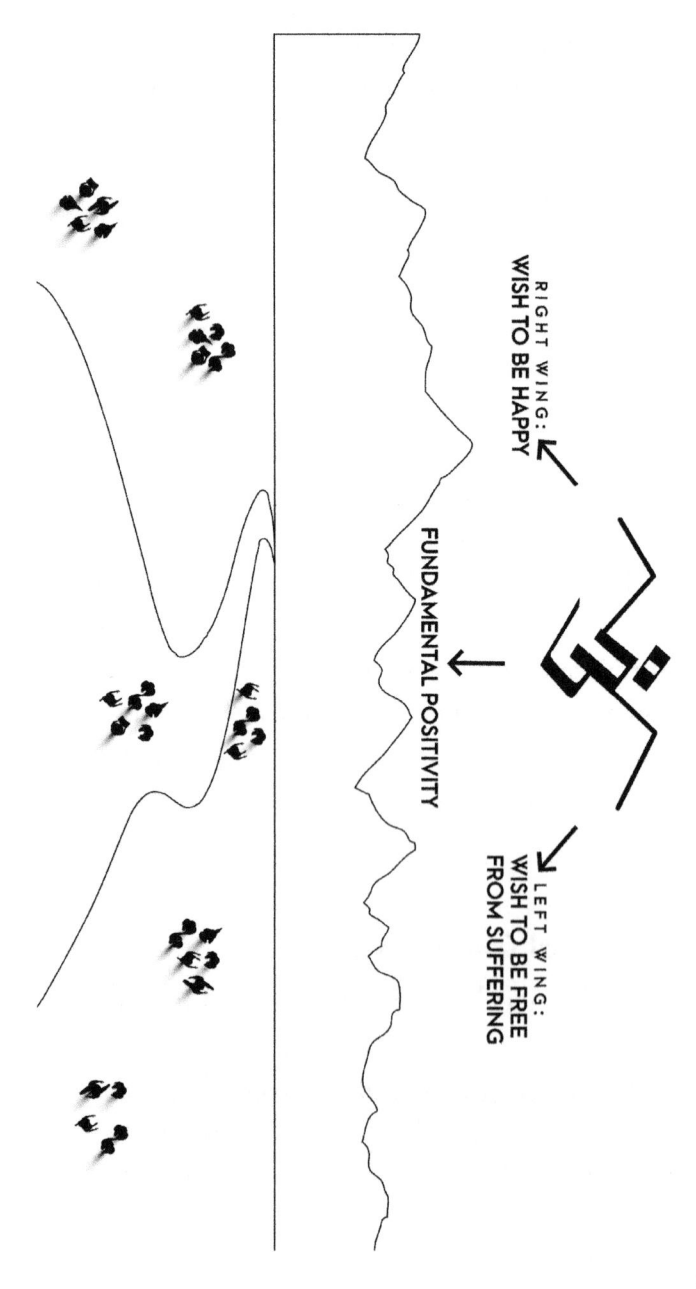

(fig.2)

Now, embodying your Fundamental Positivity, visualize yourself appearing in the aspect of this OM. Your right wing symbolizes the wish to be happy and your left wing symbolizes the wish to be free from suffering. Before you begin your flight, flap your wings and generate a genuine wish to realize happiness and be free from suffering. You have now activated your Fundamental Positivity and are ready to soar.

As you soar through the sky, observe the universe filled with sentient beings categorized into six groups: humans, demi-gods, gods, animals, hungry ghosts, and beings in hell realms. There are infinite numbers of sentient beings. Generally speaking, beings are of two kinds; sentient beings and enlightened beings. Sentient beings are those who have not developed their Fundamental Positivity to perfection, while those who have developed their Fundamental Positivity to perfection are enlightened beings. We enhance and expand our Fundamental Positivity in relation to sentient beings, not enlightened beings, because the latter have already realized ultimate happiness and have become free from suffering. Since sentient beings are infinite, our Fundamental Positivity can be enhanced infinitely. If our Fundamental Positivity is directed towards five family members it is multiplied five times; if it is directed towards a hundred friends and family members, it is multiplied a hundred times; if it is directed towards the entire population of earth, it is multiplied by seven billion, and so on. In order to realize enlightenment, we need to enhance our Fundamental Positivity infinitely, therefore the object of our Fundamental Positivity must include all sentient beings without any exclusions.

Out of the six groups, start your meditation with human beings, particularly directing your Fundamental Positivity towards loved ones beginning with those closest to your heart—your parents. Fly towards your mother, sit on her head, and gently caress her right cheek with your left wing, wishing her to be free from suffering. Then, touch her left cheek with your right wing, wishing her genuine happiness. Here, you can enhance your meditation by being specific, going through different kinds of particular sufferings and problems your mother encounters, wishing her to be free from each one of them. Then wish her various types of temporal happiness and the ultimate happiness of great nirvana. Being specific engenders clarity, intensity, and spontaneity in your meditation. Fundamental Positivity is already natural and spontaneous but, as you extend it to others, it tends to become less spontaneous. Hence the function of this vast path meditation is to make Fundamental Positivity more spontaneous as it grows and expands towards others.

Repeat the above meditation with your father, children, siblings, and other family members. Then move on to individual friends, acquaintances, co-workers, and neighbors, repeating the procedure. Fly to each person you know, sit on their head, and gently touch their cheeks with your wings, wishing them genuine happiness and freedom from suffering.

After focusing on individuals, expand your meditation to encompass larger groups such as your town, nation, and eventually all human beings throughout the universe. In this expansion of the meditation you do not need to fly to them; rather, sit where you are and just expand your wings.

At the same time wish for every being who falls under the soothing shadow of your wings to be happy and freed from suffering. Repeat the process, both individual and collective meditations for demigods, gods, animals, hungry ghosts, and beings in the hell realms. Conclude with your Fundamental Positivity embracing all sentient beings, wishing them ultimate happiness and freedom from suffering.

Measure of Realization of the Vast Path

As we continue meditating on positive realities pertaining to the Vast Path, we gradually include every being, starting from ourselves, under the two wings of Fundamental Positivity. At some point we reach a level of spontaneity extending our Fundamental Positivity to every living being, ourselves and others equally, irrespective of who they are.

At first, positive mental transformation will occur sporadically. Sometimes there will be mental transformation and other times not; our mind seems to remain rather dry. Continued training will lead to transformation that occurs reliably whenever we meditate, but not when we do not. Finally there will be a positive mental transformation of pure compassion and love that arises even without meditation. We spontaneously extend the wings of our Fundamental Positivity to every being we encounter, see, or hear of, just as we do for ourselves. When we experience this, we have reached the first level of the Vast Path. Realization of the first level of the Vast Path guarantees actualization of lasting happiness.

PROFOUND PATH

The Way to Reduce Negativity

- Identifying root negativity, cause of all negative minds
- How root negativity conceives its object
- How root negativity causes all other afflictions by conceiving the way it does
- Examining whether the conceived object can withstand a reality check
- How root negativity and derivative negativities can be eradicated if its conceived object is proven non-existent

The wisdom path deals with the root negativity which contaminates our Fundamental Positivity and gives rise to all afflicted minds such as attachment, anger, jealousy, worry, malice, fear, and so on. In the Vast Path we dealt with ways to enhance Fundamental Positivity. This automatically reduces negativity to a certain extent but to eradicate negativity completely from its root we need the Profound Path.

The Profound Path furthers what the Foundation Path and Vast Path have begun.

What is root negativity? First, Fundamental Positivity that merely wants happiness arises. This is followed by the generation of a sense of 'I.' Fundamental Positivity is then associated with 'I.' 'I want happiness,' which is still positive. Then, however, the root negativity, self-grasping, creeps in. This contaminates our sense of 'I,' turning it into self-attachment, ultimately obscuring Fundamental Positivity with a self-centered attitude.

Self-centered mind gives rise to all sorts of afflictions, including worry. It generates attachment towards people and things that we think will bring happiness. It may induce jealousy when people with whom we are angry experience happiness. Fear and all afflicted minds arise from self-centeredness which finds its root in self-grasping. Self-grasping, according to Buddha, is the root negativity. Self-grasping and its resultant self-attachment contaminate Fundamental Positivity and generate a self-centered mind within us. This is the greatest secret revealed on the Profound Path.

Self-grasping can be of two kinds: grasping the self of a living being, or grasping the self of other phenomena. The 'self' of 'self-centeredness,' however, refers to the self of a person, oneself. In the Profound Path we will identify self-grasping and then apply its antidote.

How root negativity conceives its object

Self-grasping Mind

Understanding self-grasping is critical to identifying root negativity, so I must clearly explain this particular use of the term, 'self.' Here, 'self,' 'rang' in Tibetan, means an individuality, one differentiated from others. For example, the self of a table is an individuality which distinguishes it from things that are not tables. Self is the opposite of other. Self and other are mutually exclusive. Every phenomenon in the sphere of the universe has an identity which distinguishes it from others. The question, now, is whether this self is established based on others or by itself on its own. This is the single greatest question to have ever been considered by a Buddha or anyone else!

Self-grasping mind is a mind that holds phenomena to exist from themselves, from their own side. Whenever our mind comprehends something, whether it is ourselves as a person, or something that belongs to us like a table, a book, a car, a house, it conceives it to exist independently, inherently, by itself, without depending on anything else. Terms synonymous with such 'self-existence' include 'inherent existence,' 'independently existent,' 'existing from its own side,' 'existing on its own.' Buddha asserts that our normal mind which apprehends objects as existing by themselves, independent of other factors, is the root negativity, the chief cause from which all afflicted and negative minds arise. In fact, without self-grasping as the 'mastermind,' no negative mind would arise! If we could eradicate this misconception, all negative minds would cease to exist. We tend to believe that negative minds can be reduced or destroyed temporarily but not permanently. This presents a challenge for a true inner explorer. It also comprises one of the most important aspects of Buddha's teachings.

How root negativity causes all other afflictions by conceiving the way it does

Let us analyze the mechanism by which afflictions such as attachment and anger arise. Are they rooted in self-grasping? Is it possible for negative minds or afflictive emotions such as attachment and anger to arise without self-grasping as their root cause? If this were the case, then self-grasping could not be the root cause of all negative minds; and we should not be targeting it because its destruction would not guarantee the eradication of all afflictions. It would be a futile endeavor.

There are many different causes for attachment; some are secondary causes such as beautiful objects. When our mind comes into contact with a beautiful object, we very likely become attached to it. Sometimes we build up attachment towards a beautiful object that exists only in our imagination! The same imagined beautiful object may not generate the same attachment a few days later. We might even have the opposite reaction: aversion. All of this illustrates that beautiful objects are not the primary, indispensable, cause of attachment. What is the indispensable cause of attachment and other afflictions? If we could uncover that indispensable cause, its eradication would guarantee the abandonment of all negative minds. That is our main target.

On the other hand, could negative minds all just be a part of the mind, their generation inevitable upon contact with their objects? This is the most daunting question Buddha undertook to answer. Whenever our mind apprehends a beautiful face, for instance, as existing from its own side, then there is something 'out there' for us to hang on to or grasp. Once we grasp beauty to be self-existent in this way, attachment will inevitably arise; hence, self-grasping is the indispensable cause for attachment. The same goes for all other negative minds like anger.

In this context, attachment (Tibetan, *dö chak*) is necessarily an affliction that is one of the three poisonous minds, the other two being self-grasping ignorance and aversion. There are four important elements which differentiate attachment from other similar but non-afflictive mental factors, such as wishes, desires and aspirations. These four are the causal factor, the object factor, the aspect factor, and the resultant factor. The four elements that characterize attachment are:

- The causal factor: the cause is self-grasping ignorance.
- The object factor: the object is a contaminated object.
- The aspect factor: attachment becomes entangled with its object.
- The resultant factor: attachment disturbs mental equilibrium and leads to other afflictions.

The causal factor, the underlying cause of attachment, is holding things to be self-existent. Attachment won't arise if there is no prior belief that its object is self-existent. Furthermore, objects in which attachment gets entangled must be contaminated. The wish or desire to be genuinely happy, or to want to realize Great Nirvana, is not attachment because the objects, 'genuine happiness' and 'Great Nirvana', are not contaminated objects. The object plays a major role in whether an emotion is an attachment or a desire. The nature of attachment is to become entangled or submerged in its object, like oil in paper; so much so that its intensity is disproportionate to the degree of actual pleasure derived from the object. As soon as attachment is generated, mental tranquility is lost, and other afflictive mental factors like anger and jealousy will also arise as a result. The last resultant factor distinguishes non-attachment desire such as, aspiration to free all beings from sufferings, from attachment because it doesn't lead to the loss of mental tranquility. Anger, jealousy and other derivative afflictions do not arise from it.

Identifying self-grasping in daily life

We can utilize other emotions which arise during our day to pinpoint self-grasping. For instance, if you are wrongly accused of something, the feeling of sadness or of being victimized is intense. You can feel a strong sense of 'I.' The 'I' that is blamed appears to exist from its own side, as if it has its own self-sufficient identity. Without losing this strong sense of 'I,' examine it from a corner of your mind, noticing how 'I' appears to be self-existent. Put your intellectual understanding to use in the context of your experience to identify and perceive 'self-existence' accurately, and hold on to that perception. Don't immediately analyze whether it exists or not. Do this introspective investigation repeatedly for many days until you can perceive with certainty the measure of 'self-existence' that self-grasping conceives. Imagine you are walking in a dark tunnel and bump your head on a pillar! Does it feel like the pillar is 'out there' waiting for you to bump into? Or did you bump into a pillar that exists as mere designation? If you internalize this experience, you will have a good estimation of 'self-existence,' and how perception of it influences our normal mind.

Once you are certain of this, go on to the next step: Analyze whether or not this 'self-existence' that our default mind normally apprehends actually exists. This is like having the photograph of a missing person before embarking on a mission to find them. We must have a clear estimation of the 'self-existence' conceived by self-grasping mind before we can investigate whether it can be found or not.

Examining if the conceived object can withstand a reality check

Through this process of examining our default way of perceiving things we will have gained a clear estimation of 'self-existence.' Without losing this sense of self-existence, we examine as follows: if phenomena were self-existent as they are perceived by our normal mind, it would follow that they don't depend on any other phenomenon. For example, if a table exists from itself, this implies that it doesn't depend on any other phenomenon which is not the table for its existence. Clearly this is not the case, for a table is dependent on many things that are not tables: a carpenter, the tree from which it was crafted, and so on. It is also dependent on its parts like legs, nails, and its innumerable atoms. A table can't exist if we take away its parts. There would be no table if it weren't for its legs and flat top. If a table is dependent on various non-table things, then it must be dependent on designation. If it is dependent on designation, how can it possibly exist on its own? The great Indian master Buddhapalita (5th C.) asks, 'If phenomena were to exist from their own side why would there be a need to assign them designations in dependence upon others which are not them?' We could just let them be.

How can things that are not tables come together to form a table? It is only possible when there is a designation by consciousness. If there is no involvement from a designating consciousness, how can a collection of non-tables become a table? If a table requires a designating consciousness to label a collection of things that are not a table as a table, this demonstrates that a table does not exist from its own side, by itself. If a table really existed from itself, why do parts which are non-tables and a designating consciousness (also non-table) play significant roles in establishing it? Does this not clearly show that a table exists by depending on others rather than itself?

Suppose a potential buyer is coming to purchase a horse that you advertised but you only have ten dogs in your backyard. You have two options to deal with the buyer: either tell him the truth, that there is no horse from the side of ten dogs in the backyard; or do something to his consciousness to create the illusion of a horse on the basis of ten dogs. There is no horse whatsoever from the side of the dogs, individually or collectively. This is similar to things not existing from their own side. A seller desperately seeking to get a buyer to impute 'horse' to a pack of dogs is similar to relative reality existing as mere designation upon others.

It is the coexistence of these two in all phenomena: 'absence of self-existence' and 'existence based on designation by others,' that is Buddha's greatest discovery. Within a pervasive absence of self-existent nature, all relative existence is possible, and vice versa: within all relative existence there is a pervasive absence of self-existent nature. Understanding this dynamic interplay between the two, and how they contribute to *Selwa*, the fundamental nature of mind, constitutes an understanding of Buddha's ultimate intent; nothing else!

Upon investigation by the process detailed earlier we couldn't find a self-existent table anywhere among the legs, the top, color, nails, the collection, the label, or the designator. We also realize that reality tells us something different: that a table exists in dependence on things that are not tables; and only in reliance upon consciousness as a designator. Everything that a table is dependent upon is not a table; it is 'other,' relative to the self of a table. Table simply cannot exist by itself because everything that a table is dependent upon is not a table. When a table cannot be found anywhere from its own side, we have understood emptiness. Not finding a self-existent table amounts to finding its emptiness. The thought 'Oh! This is emptiness!' is *not* the finding of emptiness. This is a finding of the relative existence of emptiness. In the actual 'finding of emptiness' we experience a mere loss or absence of the strong perception of a self-existent table that we had before, and our mind becomes like space, nothing to hold on to, no one to become attached or averse.

Not being found upon investigation makes us lose the perception of a self-existent table and experience the mere absence of a self-existent table. In this case, not finding is finding; hence, if we find something, we have not found emptiness. Emptiness is not just a theory, but an ultimate nature that pervades all phenomena equally. It is considered ultimate because there is nothing more profound, and because realizing it leads to an ultimate cessation of negativity. This is another of the great secrets revealed here.

A 'non-finding' of emptiness and the 'non-finding' of nihilism are significantly different. The non-finding of emptiness is of a self-existent table, whereas the not-finding of nihilism is of any table at all. A nihilistic approach of denying that Lady Diana is beautiful may suppress attachment, but it will not result in eradicating it because a small portion of the mind that sees the conventionally beautiful Diana may dispute it, whispering, 'That's not true!' On the other hand, once we develop a correct assessment of a self-existent beautiful Diana that is perceived by the default mind and then do not find it after a thorough search, this will lead to an experience that is like space with nothing to grasp. This can potentially eradicate attachment because it accords with reality, and no strong opponent can refute it.

The above-mentioned analysis relative to a table can be applied to all phenomena including our personal identity and abstract things like beauty. Most important to understand and meditate upon is the emptiness of 'I' since the root negativity which contaminates Fundamental Positivity is the self-grasping which perceives 'I' as self-existent.

How root negativity and derivative negativities can be eradicated if its conceived object is proven non-existent

First, it is important to have a correct estimation of how self-existence is conceived by our normal day-to-day default mind. After having a good estimation of how things appear to exist from their own side, you can investigate whether this mode of existence is compatible with other obvious and undeniable facts that you normally encounter in daily life.

So, the idea of self-existence, or existing by itself, is not compatible with many different facts. If it is not compatible with those facts, it means that self-existence does not exist. On the other hand, if it is compatible, then it does exist. This is one way of analyzing whether self-existence withstands a reality check; in other words, whether self-existence truly exists or not.

There is no denying that everything has its own 'self;' without self, there would be utter chaos and nonsense. A table is not a chair, a chair is not a table, blue is not green, round is not square, beauty is not ugly, and so on, all due to the existence of self. The self of a table makes it distinguishable from all others that are not tables. The question is not whether a table exists - we all know it does - but rather how it exists; whether it exists the way it appears to your mind or in another manner. For this, we must gain a theoretical understanding of how things would be if they existed in a self-existent way. Then, compare this theoretical perspective to your experience of grasping things, especially during moments of strong attachment, anger, or other emotional responses. Once you have a stable and reliable estimation of how things would exist if they were self-existent, compare this mode of existence with other undeniable facts such as the law of cause and effect, functionality, dependence on others, and so on. You find that they are incompatible, leading to the conclusion that all things have never ever existed by themselves. From the side of themselves, nothing exists. Everything disappears like a black hole has sucked it in, and only a mere absence of things remains. When the searching mind touches upon this mere absence, you have realized emptiness.

Dwelling in this absence, there is no room for afflictions to arise because all phenomena just disappear into emptiness when analyzed from the perspective of existing from their own side. While our minds remain focused on emptiness, no afflictions will arise. Coming out of this meditation, all phenomena miraculously reappear by means of dependence on others. During the post-meditation period, when engaging with phenomena, afflictions are reduced while positivity increases. This is a major sign that the preceding emptiness meditation had been genuine. Even though the intensity of afflictions like attachment and anger is diminished, they still linger. Therefore, in order to eradicate them completely, the initial meditative realization and subsequent understanding are not sufficient. We need to meditate further until our meditation completely merges with emptiness, becoming one with it, unveiling all dualistic appearances. When this happens, all afflictions will have been eradicated. With help of the methods that perfect Fundamental Positivity, even subtle imprints of afflictions will be destroyed. When this occurs, the highest level of lasting happiness, Great Nirvana is realized.

With respect to the emptiness of beauty, let me share my experience. Every time I see a beautiful woman's face, I let part of my awareness act as a detective to discover how the beautifulness appears. It appears as if the beautifulness is self-existent, existing in its own right; that it could not possibly be a mere designation from my mind. Firmly holding that image of self-existent beauty, I then seek it among the individual parts of the face, individually and collectively. Upon careful investigation I find nothing from the side of any part or collection of parts that represents this self-existent beauty. I also compare that image of self-existent beauty with other undeniably obvious facts such as function, cause and effect relationship, and the aspect of dependent origination. I find them incompatible as well. Subjectively, that prior, firmly-held concept of self-existent beauty dissolves, and I am left with an absence of perceiving and grasping self-existent beauty. As a consequence, my attachment gradually dissolves back into the fundamental nature of mind characterized by three attributes: clarity, emptiness, and an absence of judgment. My mind has intense clarity of awareness; it is empty in the sense of perceiving the mere absence of self-existent beauty; and calmed of developing judgmental concepts.

In the Fundamental Path I taught returning to the fundamental nature of mind through mindfulness— mere awareness. The word, 'mere,' here negates judgmental concepts. When we generate mere awareness, whether it is directed toward breathing, afflictive emotions, or awareness itself, it automatically brings our mind to its fundamental nature. Understanding emptiness and meditating on it, however, is the most profound way of bringing our mind to its fundamental nature. Arriving at the fundamental nature of mind through mindfulness alone, and by realizing emptiness, are significantly different. Mindfulness meditation only calms afflictions temporarily, whereas emptiness meditation leads to eradication of all mental afflictions. When Buddha gave teachings on emptiness during the second turning of the wheel of Dharma, he himself prepared the throne to show his disciples and future listeners like us that the teaching he was about to give was very precious and the heart of his teaching.

Wisdom Path Meditation Guide

From time immemorial we have been interacting with internal and external things. In most cases, whether these things are outside ourselves or within us, we perceive them to be self-existent, to exist from their own side without depending upon anything else. This 'self-grasping ignorance' which believes everything is self-existent is the root from which afflictions such as anger and attachment arise. They misuse our Fundamental Positivity and bring forth all varieties of suffering. Hence, self-grasping ignorance is the root of all negativity and its resultant suffering. In order to 'undo' the far-reaching negative effects of self-grasping ignorance we do analytical meditation, beginning with external things because the analysis is easier. We can use any external thing that induces a strong sense of 'mine' or 'ours:' our house, my table, my beautiful car, whatever. Let's use a table since it is one of the favorite objects of a meditator.

Relax and sit in a meditative position. Inhale deeply and exhale completely three times. Then breathe normally and meditate as follows:

This table in front of me appears to be very solid, tangible and substantial and mixed within all of its parts; yet it has its own identity as a 'table' existing from its own side distinguishing itself from all phenomena which are not table. The table appears to be existing within the collection of its parts and not elsewhere-- completely mixed together with the collection of its parts like milk poured into water-- yet it still seems to have its own identity.

Familiarize yourself with this supposed 'self-existent table,' as much you can.

Now I search for this 'self-existent table' by comparing it with other undeniable obvious facts about the table: 1. The fact that the table is dependent on infinite things which are 'not a table' such as four legs, atoms and molecules, wood and nails. 2. The fact that a bunch of 'non-table' things put together seems to miraculously become a table! 3. The fact that this 'miracle' is achieved with the help of mind designating the label, 'table,' on a collection of 'non-tables.' None of these facts are compatible with a 'self-existent table;' they are compatible with an 'other-dependent-existent' table; a table existing only in dependence upon things other than itself.

For something to exist from its own side is contradictory with its existing in dependence upon the side of 'other.' Self-existent and other-dependent-existent are mutually exclusive. Since the table exists only with the help of 'other'--- in dependence on its parts, the collection of its parts, being labeled by the mind-- how on earth could the table exist from its own side? The table has never existed on its own! (Here we have realized the emptiness of table).

My mind objects, okay, the individual parts are not the table, the mere collection of parts is not the table. However, this special collection of the parts put together that does function as a table is indeed a table! The table must exist from the side of this special collection. Therefore, it is not a mere designation.

But who first determines what is and is not the function of a table? What determines that the ability to support a coffee cup is the function of a table, not the ability to support an entire city? For ants, this 'special collection' of the table's parts could function as the latter! Thus, even the special collection is not the table. Nowhere do I find a self-existent table!

As for the world of inner phenomena, let us investigate the most prominent: the 'I' or 'me' as 'self.' Everyone has a sense of 'I,' and it appears differently in different contexts. Meditate as follows:

Sometimes the 'I' is associated with my emotions, such as when I think 'I am happy,' 'I am sad,' or 'I am angry.' Sometimes the 'I' is associated with my body, such as when I think, 'I am fat,' or 'I am thin.' Sometimes it is associated with my intelligence, such as when I think, 'I am smart,' or with my sense consciousness such as sight, when I think, 'I see the mountain.' Sometimes it is associated with the collection of both body and mind such as when someone accuses me and I think, 'Who, me?' Sometimes the 'I' seems to reside deep within my heart when I am emotionally hurt. How do I perceive the 'I' during these interactions?

At this point we just investigate without coming to any premature judgment. We allow the major part of our mind to interact in its usual way while, with a part of our mind, 'from the side,' we examine how the 'I' is being perceived during those interactions.

In all these interactions the 'I' appears to have its own concrete identity, existing from its own side, without depending on the mind that perceives it. Focusing on this 'self-existent I' that I normally perceive, without losing its sense of self-existence, I ask myself, Do I really exist in this way? Analyzing how the 'I' is dependent on many things which are not 'I,' such as my body, emotions, feelings, thinking, and so on, I conclude that the 'I' is dependent on infinite things that are not 'I.' The 'I' also depends on the consciousness that perceives it because, apart from the support of a consciousness labeling it, how does it make sense for there to be an 'I' existing amongst the many things that are 'not-I?' If the 'I' is completely dependent on the consciousness that designates it, this implies that the 'I' has never existed from its own side, 'out there' waiting to be perceived. Analyzing like this I come to the conclusion that a self-existent I is nowhere to be found. Losing the perception of a self-existent I, there is nothing to grasp or hold onto. My mind experiences an absence of the self-existent I.

We remain meditating on this emptiness of 'I' as long as the effect of the analytical process remains. If it is lost and becomes just a sense of nothingness, we repeat the entire process until the effect of the analysis is felt once again.

Measure of Realization of the Wisdom Path

Unlike the first two paths, a mere understanding of emptiness, a positive reality pertaining to this third path, constitutes realization of the wisdom path. Initially one must have a clear estimation of self-existence. Then through an analytical process of searching for it and not finding it, the mind loses its strong grasping of self-existence and becomes empty. This is the initial realization of the wisdom path. The initial realization may reduce afflictions such as attachment, anger and so forth, but it won't be an antidote that can eradicate afflictions and negativity completely. It must be further improved through continuous meditation until it becomes a union of special insight and calm-abiding mind. Then it becomes the antidote to afflictions. Once the initial realization becomes a wisdom which is a union of special insight and calm-abiding, emptiness will be realized without any dualistic appearance. The subjective wisdom and objective emptiness merge completely, so that no appearance other than emptiness arises.

(fig. 3)

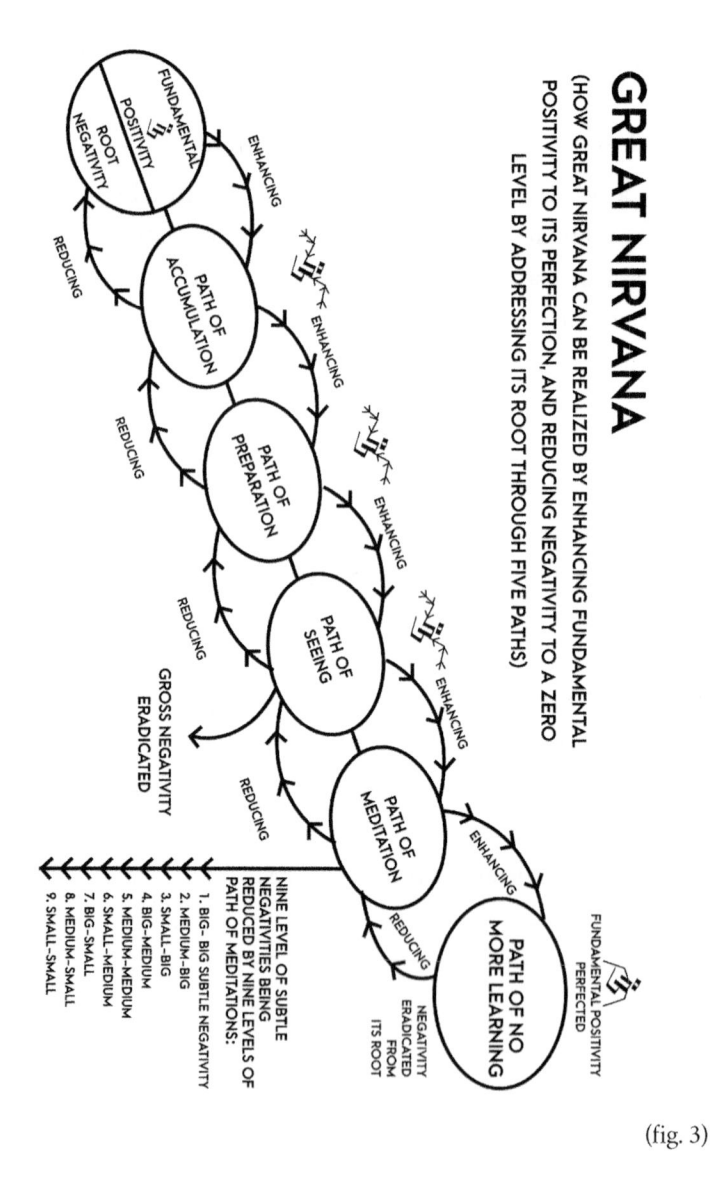

A GLIMPSE OF GREAT NIRVANA, THE PINNACLE OF LASTING HAPPINESS

During many healing sessions I have conducted over the years, clients have often asked me about the meaning of life. People seemed to be fascinated with discovering the true purpose of their lives. At first, I couldn't come up with appropriate answers. A lady once asked at the end of a session, "There must be some reason I have been born into this life! I must be here to accomplish something; what could it be?" She felt as if there were a predetermined purpose reserved for her. I had several clients ask me a similar question. After much pondering I came up with answers in two different contexts: one for clients who felt they had a predetermined purpose; and another for those who felt they had to discover the ultimate meaning of their life for themselves.

For the first, I encouraged them to be of service to others and to take good care of themselves, as well. It might be as a loving mother, a father, a lawyer, a politician, a preacher. It might be a purpose conditioned by previous karma such that they have a natural skill for it. Because it is to some extent conditioned by past karma, each individual may have a different purpose in their life. For many of us, even paying our mortgage has meaning, and it drives us to work hard.

As for the second context, in which one is seeking the ultimate meaning of life, this is paramount to deep, lasting happiness, the kind that can't be produced by external stimuli. It is a deep sense of happiness that can be present even when there are temporary problems. It is not bound by past karma; it is more related to our present actions, and is universally available to all. It is more about being an inner explorer, searching for one's true self, one's Fundamental Positivity. This is like finding one's precious inner child which, when perfected, becomes Great Nirvana.

In one healing session in Reus, Spain, I met a woman in her early fifties who, at the end of the session, asked me a question about suffering. Hers was not a superficial suffering, but rather a sense of deep, underlying suffering. She said that she had always missed being a mother. She had an abortion at a very young age and, after that, because of instability in her job and relationship, she didn't have a stable base to become a mother. And now it was too late because of her age. I said, 'Well then, since our ritual healing session is over, would you like to discuss this in a longer session with me?" She gladly agreed, and I initiated the conversation by asking "Since you couldn't have in the past, and cannot now, then why don't you take care of a child which you already have?" To her raised eyebrows and widened eyes I introduced her to her Fundamental Positivity, her inner child. Over the course of three sessions, I explained how it could be cared for, nourished, and blossom into Great Nirvana. I described how negativity is like the spoiling of the inner child, how it can be reduced, and finally dissolved back into the inner child of Fundamental Positivity. I briefly introduced the five paths leading to Great Nirvana, and at the end of our third session she said was quite happy. She commented that she had understood Fundamental Positivity, but had not well understood negativity, how it could be reduced and permanently dissolved. I told her that I had given her just a glimpse of Great Nirvana, an introduction to its precious meaning. Being a mother held great meaning for her, so to compensate for her loss I introduced her to an even greater meaning; anything less would not have sufficed. Then I told her that if she wanted to go beyond that glimpse, comprehensive study with a qualified Buddhist master would be essential.

There are two nirvanas expounded in Buddhist scriptures: Small Nirvana and Great Nirvana. Small nirvana is a state of being in which Fundamental Positivity has not been enhanced to perfection, and negativity has been eradicated only partially; its subtle imprint still remains. Those who attain small Nirvana are called Arhats.

Great Nirvana, the highest level of lasting happiness known as Buddhahood is the ultimate spiritual destination. It requires that Fundamental Positivity be enhanced to perfection; and not only gross negativity but its subtle imprint must be eradicated as well. Since we have now understood Fundamental Positivity, and the root of negativity, the possibility of Great Nirvana is easy to establish, at least in theory. We shouldn't belittle even a theoretical understanding of Great Nirvana because it can provide a sense of ultimate meaning for our life. The theoretical understanding that the ultimate realization of Great Nirvana can be achieved by diligently developing our Fundamental Positivity to its fullest potential, while simultaneously eliminating negativity to a state of complete absence, is known as Nirvana Wisdom. The benefit of Nirvana Wisdom is that it is easier to acquire than Great Nirvana itself; and even on a theoretical level it can provide a deep sense of peace and comfort. Here I present a glimpse of Great Nirvana so that the reader may have a foundation on which actual Nirvana Wisdom can soon be built. This requires a college-like education at an institute such as the Buddhist Academy which I will soon be founding. Since this is just a glimpse, I have avoided technical terms and more details that are presented in the traditional scriptures. Moreover, I will present the five paths leading to Great Nirvana in a manner that is common to both Buddhist Sutra and Tantra.

We are all sentient beings and possess consciousness or mind. Within our consciousness we have two potentials: positive and negative. All positivity can be attributed to basic positivity which is fundamental and naturally within us. Negativity, whether in action or mental afflictions like attachment, anger, and jealousy, can be traced back to the root of all negativity: self-grasping ignorance. Both Fundamental Positivity and negativity exist in consciousness but in a different manner. Fundamental Positivity exists in the very nature of the mind, while negativity is adventitious and can be removed. If we enhance our Fundamental Positivity to the level of perfection, and reduce negativity to zero, never to arise again, then our consciousness has reached the state of Great Nirvana. This could be the best summarization of Great Nirvana, Buddhahood or Enlightenment, whatever you wish to call it.

There are five paths, actually five stages of the path, that lead to Great Nirvana:

> Path of Accumulation *(Tsok-lam)*
> Path of Preparation *(Jor-lam)*
> Path of Seeing *(Thong-lam)*
> Path of Meditation *(Gom-lam)*
> Path of No More Training *(Milob-lam)*

Path of Accumulation

Prior to realizing the path of accumulation, we are ordinary beings striving to nourish and enhance Fundamental Positivity through every possible positive action. Accumulation of even a small positive act such as smiling at our coworker when we greet them in the morning will enhance and nourish our Fundamental Positivity. We are not only being kind to our coworker but to ourselves as well, since we are nurturing our inner child. A simple act of generosity, giving a dollar to a needy person; the good deed of picking up a dog's waste; having patience for drivers who honk needlessly; feeling enthusiastic about doing even small good deeds; all these positive actions can nourish and enhance our Fundamental Positivity. In a nutshell, no positive action is too large or too small to enhance our Fundamental Positivity. However, for the path of accumulation, a systematic approach of enhancing our Fundamental Positivity must be employed: this is the Bodhicitta mind training. Bodhicitta is a special mind that excels as the best method to nourish Fundamental Positivity. Arya Vimuktisena (6th C.) in his commentary on Abhisamayalamkara, the classic text on the Buddhist path to enlightenment, states that since Bodhicitta is oriented towards all positive phenomena, it is the inexhaustible source of all positivity.

There are two systems of mind training which come from Buddha through two different lineages. One, called 'equalization and exchange of self with others,' reaches us through the lineage of the Indian master, Nagarjuna; and the other, known as 'seven-fold cause and effect' came through the Indian master, Asanga. Both methods are excellent for enhancing Fundamental Positivity and eventually transforming it into Bodhicitta. Once a meditator has transformed his or her Fundamental Positivity into actual Bodhicitta through mind training methods, the meditator has realized the first path, the "Path of Accumulation." The 12th century Tibetan meditator, Geshe Chekawa, is said to have taken only six months to transform his Fundamental Positivity into actual Bodhicitta. In order to reach Buddhahood, Fundamental Positivity must be perfected, and Bodhicitta is the indispensable method for it. Without the help of Bodhicitta, Fundamental Positivity cannot be perfected; and without Fundamental Positivity reaching its perfected level, Buddhahood is not possible. Hence, the great Indian master Nagarjuna (2nd C.) proclaimed, "You who want to reach unsurpassable Buddhahood! Know that Bodhicitta is the root!"

Nothing can beat Bodhicitta when it comes to enhancing Fundamental Positivity. A person who has realized Bodhicitta (who has transformed their Fundamental Positivity into Bodhicitta) has officially entered the Great Nirvana path, and has actualized authentic lasting happiness.

There is a debate in classical Buddhist texts about whether a happy migration must necessarily be human, demi-god, or god (the worldly gods of Hindu & Buddhist mythology). The 17th century Tibetan master Jamyang Shepa argued that since Bodhicitta can be generated in an animal existence, such an animal can be classified as a happy migration even though it is none of the three, human, demi-god or god. His main argument is that if Bodhicitta is generated in any being, they have realized lasting happiness and will only go from happiness to happiness. Although happiness is limited by an animal's state, Bodhicitta is so powerful that it can, very occasionally, even transform animal existence into a happy migration!

Here I sincerely request that those readers who strive to enhance their Fundamental Positivity to the level of perfection (Buddhahood) seek the path of Bodhicitta mind training under the guidance of a qualified teacher. For others, you may enhance your Fundamental Positivity by means of any positive action, regardless of religious affiliations, and beliefs.

Path of Preparation

Having reached the path of accumulation, in which we have realized our Fundamental Positivity and transformed it into Bodhicitta, we have an inexhaustible source for positivity. Positivity within us keeps increasing and accumulating even while we are asleep. So we have nurtured our positivity to a great extent. However, while increasing and enhancing positivity *does*, indirectly, reduce negativity, it does not address the root negativity. Hence, we now focus on eliminating negativity permanently by addressing its root. Since self-grasping ignorance is the root cause of negativity, eradicating it will lead to permanent freedom from all negativity. Self-grasping ignorance must first be reduced gradually from its grosser to more subtle forms. In its gross form it is the mind which grasps phenomena as truly existent, while in its subtle form it is the latent potency leftover from that grasping which predisposes phenomena to *appear* as if they truly existed.

The antidote to the gross level of self-grasping ignorance is the Path of Seeing, and the antidote to the subtle level is the Path of Meditation. The paths of Seeing and Meditation are the actual paths that permanently eradicate negativity from its root. Reaching these two paths requires a great deal of preparation through learning, contemplation and meditation in order to understand the ultimate nature of reality. Hence, the path of preparation comes into play. On the path of preparation, we try to discover how things exist, not only how they appear on the surface, but how they actually exist in their depths, ultimately. We find that phenomena are empty of self-existence, in direct contradiction to the ignorance which grasps them as self-existent. In the beginning we understand emptiness theoretically, through learning and contemplation. Once we understand emptiness correctly by means of learning and contemplation, without stopping there, we then continue by meditating using two methods: single-pointedness and investigation.

Although we have now understood emptiness theoretically, during our meditation session we deepen our investigation and, as a result, we come to the conclusion:

"Things are empty of self-existence." We then place our focus single-pointedly on that conclusion. We keep on alternating these two types of meditation-- 1. detailed investigation of emptiness, and 2. placing our mind single-pointedly on our arrived conclusion-- until we reach a point at which we don't need to depend on inner dialogue to grasp the meaning of emptiness. Here we have reached the actual state of meditation on emptiness. Prior to this we were meditating, but our meditation had not yet become actual meditation. Our understanding was only theoretical, and whenever theoretical understanding comprehends emptiness, it must go through a mental process of saying something to ourselves about it, describing the object that we seek to comprehend. Through continuing the process, we reach a point at which we no longer depend on mentally reciting the word, 'emptiness,' and its related details, but touch the meaning of emptiness, directly. At that point we are actually meditating on emptiness. We continue the meditation and reach a point at which our meditation on emptiness becomes quite advanced. When we experience a special, blissful pliancy in our meditation, coming not only from single-pointed meditation as it did before, but even when we merely turn our mind to the analytical meditation, then we have passed from the path of accumulation to the path of preparation. On the path of preparation, we initiate a process that will eliminate negativity completely by unifying calm abiding with special insight. Calm abiding is the culmination of single-pointed meditation, and special insight is the culmination of investigative meditation.

The path of preparation has four divisions based on how it cuts through dualistic appearances before reaching the path of seeing, directly realizing emptiness non-conceptually.

Four Divisions of the Path of Preparation

- Heat
- Peak
- Patience
- Supreme Phenomena

Heat

When we pass from the path of accumulation to the path of preparation our meditation on *shunyata* (emptiness) has reached an advanced level. During the stage of theoretical understanding there was a gross dual appearance of a separate subject (the meditating mind) and its object *(shunyata)*. There was a sense of distance between the subject 'in here,' and the object 'out there.' During the heat stage of the path of preparation, this dualistic appearance has diminished, but the meditator still experiences a subtle duality with the object, which at this point is still just a mental image of *shunyata*. The realization of this image, however, marks the beginning of the heat level of the path of preparation. It is called 'heat' because the meditator has reached close enough to the fire of the Path of Seeing that its heat can be felt.

Peak

As we continue to meditate on emptiness the dualistic appearance diminishes even more. The meditator can still feel a separateness of subject and object but the realization of emptiness has grown clearer. At this advanced stage of realizing emptiness, negativity has been weakened to such a degree that mental afflictions like anger can no longer shake the meditator's positive foundation; they have reached a peak of unshakable positivity.

Patience

As we continue to meditate, dualistic appearances diminish even more until we are absorbed so intensely in emptiness that we experience only the subjective viewer, without the sense of there being an appearing object. The mind is so absorbed in emptiness that it no longer feels the 'existence' of emptiness; it does, however, still feel the 'existence' of a meditating mind. A person on the patience stage of the path of preparation has reached a very high level of clarity realizing emptiness. They are immensely comfortable and patient to persevere in their understanding, and they become free from all fear of emptiness. At this stage their past negative karma can no longer ripen in lower realm rebirth.

Supreme Phenomena

Through our meditative stabilization utilizing calm-abiding and special insight we continue to meditate on emptiness and reach a point at which we don't experience even the 'existence' of a subjective mind. It seems as if all dualistic appearance has disappeared. At this point we have realized the ultimate clarity of a mental image of emptiness. Here, the meditator is on the last stage of being an ordinary person; the supreme state of an ordinary being.

Path of Seeing

Continuing to meditate on emptiness on the level of Supreme Phenomena, when the layer of even subtle dualistic appearance is peeled away completely and we directly perceive emptiness without any mental image, we reach the glorious Path of Seeing. We become an Arya being. Until then, we have been an ordinary being. Upon reaching the Path of Seeing we have almost completely eradicated the gross level of negativity and its resultant sufferings of birth, sickness, aging and death.

According to the Buddhist tantric system, a practitioner on the path of seeing uses his or her subtlest mind of clear light to perceive emptiness directly while experiencing great bliss. Great bliss is generated automatically as a result of the process gone through on the tantric path of preparation, in which the practitioner has gained complete control of their clear light mind. The energy-wind which the clear light mind is mounted upon is the subtlest energy-wind, and it is of one nature with the clear light mind. It is considered the most precious physical matter because it is the substantial cause of the Illusory Body. When the practitioner finally arises from their meditative equipoise they find another body, like an astral body, created within their gross body of flesh and bone. It is an indestructible body which will finally put an end to the round of birth, death and bardo, because a person who has actualized Illusory Body is guaranteed to realize the fully enlightened state in that very lifetime.

To clarify the difference between gross wind and subtle energy-wind, gross wind is the movement of the air we breathe; it functions to blow things away. Energy-wind is a subtle wind that does not blow away other physical things; rather, it moves consciousness to function. The energy or vibratory force that moves or 'blows' our consciousness to its object is called an energy-wind.

There are some famous lines on this subject by the great Indian master

Aryadeva (3rd C.):

There are four elements, earth, [water, fire, and wind]
and four aspects of emptiness,
which should be known as eight phenomena
which are the basis of our creation and disintegration.

His continuing explanation of these words is rather cryptic, so I will paraphrase it in plain language as follows.

As we are gaining experience of the clear light mind realization of emptiness and the experience of our body has disappeared, there is a process which occurs when the experience of our body and physical world reemerges. First, there are four aspects of emptiness which arise: clear light mind, black empty mind, red empty mind, and white empty mind. As the process continues, four elements arise: wind, fire, water, and earth. Then, when we meditate on emptiness, our body and the physical world again seem to disappear and the process is reversed. Earth dissolves into water, water into fire, fire into wind, wind into white empty mind, white into red empty mind, red into black empty mind, and black into clear light mind. Black empty mind actually has two phases: a conscious black empty mind followed by an unconscious black empty mind. With the dissolution of the unconscious black empty mind into clear light mind, we reach a consciousness devoid of any conceptual thought, irreducible, uncontrived, which has existed ceaselessly since beginningless time.

Aryadeva says that it is this realization which brings an end to the suffering of uncontrolled cyclic death and rebirth. He concludes by saying,

> The wheel of unenlightened existence,
> which has no beginning in time,
> will keep on spinning
> until the Illusory Body samadhi is realized.

Path of Meditation

Once we have seen *shunyata*, the ultimate mode of reality, directly, without any dualistic appearance of a mental image, we must still continue to meditate on *shunyata* in order to eradicate subtle negativity. As mentioned before, self-grasping ignorance which perceives phenomena as self-existent is the gross root negativity, while its imprint or latent potency left in our consciousness is subtle negativity. Once we have reached the Arya state of the path of seeing, we will no longer have self-grasping ignorance, the gross negativity; nevertheless, objects will still appear to be self-existent due to the imprints we carry from our previous self-grasping ignorance. These imprints are what block our mind from perceiving all phenomena simultaneously.

When a magician casts a spell on a stone and transforms it into a horse, onlookers will have the appearance of a real horse, and will also believe it is a real horse. The magician, on the other hand, doesn't believe that there is a real horse, but still sees the image of the horse he is creating as if it was truly there. This is like an Arya being who has eliminated gross negativity but still has the latent appearance of true existence. Even without believing it, just seeing the false appearance of self-existence is still a subtle form of negativity. We must train in the path of meditation to gradually eradicate subtle negativity. Subtle negativity is divided into nine levels: three graded levels of least subtlety, three levels of medium subtlety, and three levels of finest subtlety. They are known as big-big, medium-big and small-big; big-medium, medium-medium, and small-medium; and big-small, medium-small, and small-small. These nine levels of subtle negativity are eradicated on nine levels of the path of meditation. The final, ninth level, known as the vajra-like meditative stabilization, is the direct antidote to the subtlest negativity, the small-small. The Tantric level path of meditation is the clear light mind that has the power to eradicate the subtlest negativity. The subtlest energy-wind associated with this clear light mind is the substantial cause of the Illusory body and the Sambhogakaya, the 'body of enjoyment,' of a fully enlightened being.

It should be noted, however, that while it is the direct antidote, it is wholly dependent upon all that has previously contributed to its realization, especially our Fundamental Positivity having been transformed into bodhicitta. *Shunyata* has been realized already, but for it to become the antidote to subtle negativity depends upon its further integration with continuing development of aspects of the Vast Path. The ever-increasing power of bodhicitta enables wisdom realization to become the direct antidote to subtlest negativity-- the obstructions to omniscience.

Path of No-More-Training

When we are on the ninth level of the path of meditation our status as a sentient being is in its final stage. We are moments away from full enlightenment. Our vajra-like path of meditation realizes *shunyata* with complete absorption. This ninth level of the path of meditation is also referred to as 'Illusory Body samadhi' as great master Aryadeva pointed out before. Nothing other than *shunyata* is perceived. With its continuation, small-small subtle negativity is completely eliminated. When this happens, what was previously the path of meditation, fully absorbed in emptiness and nothing else, now perceives all phenomena simultaneously, while still realizing their ultimate nature, their emptiness.' At this point we reach the Path of No More Training, Buddhahood, Great Nirvana. Our Fundamental Positivity has reached perfection! The tiniest trace of negativity has been reduced to zero! Welcome to the land of Buddha! Yahooooooooooo! Congratulations on the coronation of Fundamental Positivity!

Glossary

Abhisamayalamkara Ornament of Clear Realization; classic text on the Buddhist path to enlightenment by Maitreya.

Asanga Fourth century Indian Buddhist philosopher-adept who founded Yogachara school of Buddhism.

analytical meditation Meditation which focuses on details or constituent parts of a meditative object.

anger Strong emotion of annoyance, irritation, etc.

animals One of the six realms according to Buddhist cosmology.

anxiety Feeling of nervousness, unease.

Arya Sanskrit. A person who has direct realization of shunyata, from the path of seeing onwards.

Aryadeva Third century Indian monk-philosopher; an important source of madhyamaka philosophy; author of the Four Hundred Verses on the Middle Way.

attachment Tibetan, do-chak. In this context, necessarily afflictive, involving exaggeration of positive qualities, as well as craving and clinging. One of the three poisonous delusions of ignorance, attachment, and aversion. Four factors which differentiate attachment from non-afflictive forms of desire, wishes, and aspirations are:

    causal factor   self-grasping ignorance;
    object factor   a contaminated object;
    aspect factor   attachment becomes fused with its object;
    resultant factor   mental equilibrium is disturbed, leading to other afflictions.

beginningless time When Buddha attained the omniscience of full awakening, he said that he saw all of his previous lives, but that there was no beginning to them, they stretched back into infinity.

bodhicitta The wish for complete enlightenment in order to bring happiness to all living beings. It ranges from being generated through effort, to becoming uncontrived, continuous, and effortless. The best method to nourish fundamental positivity.

buddha Buddha is a fully enlightened, fully awakened being, endowed with universal love, omniscient mind and every possible capacity to benefit others; who has eliminated all internal faults and deficiencies and has developed all possible internal good qualities, who has attained the state of Buddhahood. The historical Buddha lived over 2500 years ago.

buddhahood The state attained by a Buddha.

buddha-mind Completely pure mind. Selwa of ordinary beings is temporarily obscured by negativity, whereas Selwa of Buddha-mind is free of all negativity and obscuration.

Buddhapalita Fifth-sixth century Indian Philosopher associated with the Prasangika school of Madhyamaka. Main disciple of Nagarjuna.

buddhist tenet systems Systems of philosophy in Buddhism which present the relative and ultimate natures of phenomena.

Chandrakirti Seventh century Indian philosopher-adept who wrote on the Middle Way, Sanskrit. Madhyamaka. Trailblazer of Madhyamaka Prasangika school.

chuba Traditional Tibetan attire, a warm knee-length robe.

cognitions Understandings, which can be valid or invalid, which give rise to feelings and emotions.

compassion The wish for oneself and others to be free from suffering.

default mind Mind in its uncontrolled state, left in its usual, habitual mode of experience and reaction.

demi-gods One of the six realms according to Buddhist cosmology. Celestial beings who compete and war with the gods.

designation by consciousness Labeling a phenomenon on a collection of its parts, basis of designation.

deep suffering Suffering occurs more on a mental level caused by missing out on a deeper meanings.

discernment Understanding of meanings, which leads to thought.

discrimination In a negative sense, between one's own and others' happiness, with one's own being more important than others'.

Dharmakirti Sixth-seventh century Indian philosopher who wrote Commentary on Valid Cognition, Pramanavarttika.

dualistic appearance Sense of distance between subject and object involving mental imaging.

emotional mind In this context, responses to experiences of pleasant, unpleasant, and neutral feelings.

emotionalizing Developing emotions in reaction to feelings.

feelings Experiences of pleasure, displeasure, or neutral feelings; which lead to wishes and emotions.

foundation path Identifying the mind's mere clarity of awareness and its Fundamental positivity, and undoing the misuse of Fundamental positivity by default mind.

four Noble Truths
  Suffering which is to be recognized.
  Causes of Suffering which are to be Eliminated.
  Cessation of Suffering which is to be Actualized.
  Path to Cessation of Suffering, which is to be Practiced.

geluk literally The virtuous tradition, the school of Tibetan Buddhism which evolved from the teachings of Je Tsongkhapa.

gen Tibetan. Teacher.

Gen Lamrimpa Contemporary Tibetan meditation teacher (1936-2004), the author's root guru.

Gen Nyima Jorlampa (a person who has reached the path of preparation) the late contemporary Tibetan Tantric Yogi who stayed in solitary retreat in Bhutan for many years; who became a highly realized great adept and healer. Author's guru.

geshe The title given a Tibetan Buddhist monk after completing study of five topics: Abhidharma (Compendium of Scriptural Knowledge), Vinaya (Discipline), Madhyamaka (Middle Way Philosophy), Pramana (Valid Cognition), and Prajnaparamita (Perfection of Wisdom).

Geshe Chekawa Twelfth century Tibetan meditation master who wrote the Seven-Point Mind Training.

gods One of the six realms according to Buddhist cosmology, celestial beings of various levels.

great nirvana The state of full enlightenment, in which the root negativity has been eliminated and Fundamental positivity has been perfected.

gross mind Normal waking mind of thinking and discernment; most feelings and emotions. When it becomes very stable and clear gross mind can transform into subtle mind.

Guhyasamaja A meditational Deity of Father Tantra of Highest Yoga Tantra.

Guru Sanskrit, Tibetan. Lama   a spiritual master or teacher.

happiness   The experience of pleasant, positive feelings, what we naturally want
> when derived from external phenomena: temporary, materially-creatable, conditional, dependent, superficial, suffering of change;
> when arising internally, from within the mind, itself: lasting, genuine, reliable, non-dependent, non-materially-creatable, unconditional.

His Holiness the Dalai Lama   Contemporary spiritual head of Tibetan Buddhism, currently in the Fourteenth incarnation of his lineage.

hells   One of the six realms according to Buddhist cosmology, realms of intense suffering of violence, heat, cold, etc.

Heruka Chakrasamvara   Meditational deity of mother Tantra of highest yoga Tantra.

humans   One of the six realms according to Buddhist cosmology, human beings. Attained primarily through karma of keeping ethical discipline.

hungry ghosts   One of the six realms according to Buddhist cosmology, spirits trapped in realms of deprivation.

illusory body Tibetan. gyu-lu   An astral body within the gross body formed from the subtlest energy-wind, mount of the clear-light mind, which manifests at highly realized levels of meditation. When realized, it destroys the cycle of death, intermediate state, and rebirth.

illusory body samadhi   Meditative equipoise of Tantric Path of Seeing that is the union of great bliss and subtlest mind of clear light. This union is generated as a result of Tantric Path of Preparation. All Tantric Path of Meditations are also this Samadhi.

invalid cognition   Superimposition of the existence of something which does not exist, or exaggeration or denial of something which does exist.

Jadrel Tibetan.   A renounced meditator, one who has given up all mundane works and activities.

Jampa Yeshi   Abbot emeritus of Ganden Shartse monastery, the author's root guru.

Jamyang Shepa   Seventeenth century Tibetan master who wrote on philosophical tenet systems, which are studied in Drepung Gomang Monastery.

Je Tsongkhapa   (1357–1419) Tibetan ordained master whose study, practice and realization of Buddha's teachings led to the development of the Geluk tradition of Tibetan Buddhism.

jealousy   The emotion of being unhappy about others' happiness or good qualities.

karma   Action, physical, verbal, and mental; mental being the most important. These actions leave imprints in our mind which eventually ripen and give rise to our future state of being.

karmic causality   Natural law of karma, how mind gives rise to all phenomena. Everything comes from causes, nothing happens without a cause.

Lati Rinpoche   Abbot emeritus of Ganden Shartse Monastery, the author's root guru.

love   The wish for oneself and others to be happy.

Mani pill   A small pellet highly blessed with many recitations of the Mantra of Avalokitesvara, OM MANI PADME HUM.

Manjugoshaya Sanskrit   The Buddha/Bodhisattva who embodies and bears the profound, wisdom teachings of the Buddhas.

measure of meditation   Gauging when meditation becomes actual or true meditation, not just a mental exercise. Meditation can yield observable effects on feelings and emotion only when it becomes actual meditation, when the mind has become stable and clear enough to penetrate and dissolve into its object, as if becoming one with the object.

meditation   A universally practical and active method for experiencing happiness that is not generated from objects of the senses. Path of the inner world of the mind.

memory   The link between all mental factors, connecting past mind to present mind. Like an imprint laid down by the mind.

Milarepa   Famous eleventh century Tibetan Yogi; renowned for having attained enlightenment during his lifetime and expressing his realizations in songs.

mind Our inner world, in its basic nature, mere awareness and clarity. As a category, it encompasses all types of consciousness and mental activity.

misconception of self Grasping a misconceived sense of self, a self that is independently or inherently existent, existing from its own side. Such a conceived object is investigated to find out if it actually exists in accordance with how it is perceived.

mother sentient beings All conscious beings with an understanding of them all having been one's mother during the infinite timeline of reincarnation.

Nagarjuna 2nd century Indian Buddhist Philosopher-adept who propounded Madhyamika school system, and wrote extensive commentarial texts on Wisdom of Perfection Sutra.

Namgyal Dratsang His Holiness the Fourteenth Dalai Lama's private monastery.

namo Sanskrit An expression of homage or praise.

negative mind Mind with negative aspect and potential, caused by a misconception of self-grasping mind.

negativity Cause of suffering, having the potential to give rise to suffering.

nihilism A mistaken belief in the non-existence of things which are not seen.

nirvana Liberation from the round of reincarnation driven by ignorance, afflictive emotions, and the derivative karmic causes and effects. The state of mind free of at least the grosser level of obscuration— deluded obscurations which grasp the appearance of inherent existence of phenomena as true.

nirvana wisdom Conviction based on three wisdoms (derived from learning, contemplation and meditation) that nirvana is possible within oneself.

non-conceptual mind Sense consciousnesses and direct mental perception, without mental imagery and labels.

object In the context of meditation, a positive object to be meditated upon.

objects In a general context: objects of mind; may be positive, negative, or neutral.

other-dependent existence Phenomena existing in dependence on other factors.

parinirvana The death or passing away of a highly realized spiritual practitioner or enlightened being; actually, their withdrawal from the grosser level of emanation.

path of accumulation A path of spiritual development which nourishes fundamental positivity by accumulating causes for enlightenment with a motivation of bodhicitta.

path of meditation Along with the path of seeing, the path which actually eradicates negativity from its root.

path of no-more-training Buddhahood, Great Nirvana.

path of preparation A path of spiritual development which begins to focus on permanently eliminating negativity by eradicating its root, self-grasping ignorance.

path of seeing   The third path, which eradicates gross negativity from its root.

perception   Taking in the appearance of objects without grasping, which leads to thought.

placement meditation   Meditation which focuses on the whole spectrum of a meditative object. Holding the mind single-pointedly focused on an object, for example, that every living being has Fundamental positivity.

positivity   Positive potential, causes of happiness, positive realities, having the potential to give rise to happiness.

profound path   The way to reduce negative, disturbed minds, by eliminating the root negativity, self-grasping ignorance, and its associated self-centered attitude.

Rigpa   Mere awareness or knowing, which allows for reflection, perception, discernment, thought, feeling, wishing, emotionalizing, etc.

sadness   Mental suffering, an afflictive emotion, a feeling which may arise when temporary happiness ceases.

Sambhogakaya Sanskrit.   The 'Body of Enjoyment' the wisdom-light body which is the perfected evolvement of the Illusory Body.

self-centered attitude   A polluted form of the Fundamental positivity which considers one's freedom of suffering and realization of one's own happiness more important than those of others'.

self-existence   Phenomena existing independently, from their own side.

self-grasping   The active form of ignorance which clings to a fantasized or projected sense of self as self-existent.

Selwa   clarity, The fundamental nature of mind which has two components: Fundamental positivity and Emptiness.

Shantideva   Eighth century Indian philosopher-adept who wrote Bodhicaryavatara, the Guide to the Bodhisattva Conduct, and Siksasamuccaya, The Compendium of Training.

shunyata Sanskrit   Emptiness or selflessness, in this context, ultimate fundamental nature of mind, and the ultimate nature of self and other phenomena, lacking independent, self-existence.

subject   In the context of meditation, the mind which meditates.

subtle mind   More powerful than gross mind; the results from training the gross mind to perceive with more intensity. Also manifests during sleep. From the time of conception, the mind first manifests in its subtlest form, then becomes subtle, then gross, then very gross.

subtlest mind   Corresponding to Western idea of spirit or soul. In the context of Buddhist Tantra, clear light mind, extending from infinite time past to infinite time in the future.

suffering   The experience of unpleasant, negative feelings, what we naturally don't want.

superficial suffering   Suffering on sensorial level, mental disturbance on the surface level of mind primarily caused by typical daily mundane problems.

suffering of change Temporary relief from suffering, contaminated samsaric happiness which changes into suffering.

sutrayana Exoteric teachings of Buddha categorized in four philosophical tenet systems as formulated in Tibetan Buddhism.

sensory mind Sense consciousnesses, visual, audial, olfactory, gustatory, and tactile consciousnesses which arise in dependence upon the sense faculties and external stimulation.

tantrayana The esoteric Teachings of Buddhadharma, compared to taking a rocket ship to enlightenment!

thought Conceptual minds, (more superficial than feelings), which find ideas and words suitable to be associated with each other; which leads to feelings

three great monasteries in south India Drepung, Sera, and Ganden.

tulku Tibetan. The recognized reincarnation of a spiritual practitioner. Literally, an 'emanation body.' In the case of Buddhahood or Great Nirvana, the Nirmanakayas of full enlightenment.

vajra Sanskrit Symbol of indestructibility, power, and clarity.

vajra-like meditative stabilization The most powerful meditation which immediately precedes full enlightenment, which eliminates the most subtle level of negativity.

valid cognition Understanding phenomena in accordance with their mode of existence.

vast path Spiritual development which extends and expands fundamental positivity.

Vimuktisena Sixth century Indian commentator on the Abhisamayalamkara.

walking the inner path After perceiving positive realities, continuously meditating on them in order to engender positive transformation.

wishing Desires in reaction to cognitions and feelings.

worry An emotion of mental disturbance which results from misuse of fundamental positivity.

Yamantaka A meditational deity of highest yoga tantra, wrathful form of Manjushri, Buddha of wisdom.

Acknowledgments

I am thrilled to bring to you "The Tibetan Book of Happiness", a work that is very dear to my heart and a result of many years of personal exploration and introspection. This journey, however, was not embarked upon alone and there are a few special individuals to whom I owe heartfelt gratitude.

Firstly, I want to express my deepest appreciation to my teachers at the monastery. Their guidance, compassion and wisdom have been my ultimate refuge. This book is merely a reflection of the profound insights they generously bestowed and the profound lessons I learned during my time studying under them.

Next, I would like to acknowledge my editor, Jampa Tharchin. His expertise and diligence made this book the best it could be while preserving its informal essence. His skillful editing touch ensured that the originality and spontaneity of my writing were maintained, allowing the book to remain true to my original vision.

Lastly, but certainly not least, to you, the reader, I extend my sincere thanks. This book was written with the hope of sharing the beauty and depth of Tibetan wisdom on happiness with you. I hope that in its pages you will find tools and insights that inspire you to explore your own path to happiness.

In keeping with Tibetan traditions, my aspiration is for this book to act as a beacon of light for anyone seeking to uncover the true essence of happiness

THE BADAWA ACADEMY CURRICULUM AND ITS MISSION

At the heart of the Badawa Academy's curriculum lies a noble mission: to engender Nirvana Wisdom within the minds of our students. This wisdom is not merely an abstract concept but a profound wisdom of enlightenment that can infuse life with profound meaning and dispel the shadows of mental suffering.

Nirvana Wisdom, as imparted by the Badawa Academy, has the power to:
- Illuminate the path to genuine, lasting fulfillment.
- Offer clarity and purpose in the face of life's complexities.
- Alleviate the burdens of mental anguish and emotional turmoil.

The Badawa Academy Curriculum

Our curriculum is meticulously crafted to guide you on this transformative journey. It encompasses:
1. Collected Topics: "A Jewel Lamp to Illuminate the Characteristics of Phenomena" by Great Tibetan master Badawa. A foundation that serves as the key to unlocking the profound meanings of Buddhist scriptures. It offers a solid footing upon which to build your spiritual exploration.

2. Lamrim, the Stages of the Path to Enlightenment: These extraordinary instructions, originally composed by the Indian master Atisha, provide a practical roadmap for progressing on the Buddhist path—from its inception to its culmination. It is a guide to genuine spiritual growth.
3. Abhisamayalankara, the Ornament for Clear Realization: This extensive presentation of the Lamrim reveals the hidden meanings within the Perfection of Wisdom Sutras. It offers a detailed description of the ascending stages of realization attained through meditation on emptiness. As you study the Ornament for Clear Realization, the Lamrim becomes a potent meditation manual, exponentially enhancing its effectiveness and power.
4. Tantra: Our curriculum places special emphasis on the practice of the Six Yogas of Naropa. You will explore a comprehensive presentation that covers all essential instructions of the Father and Mother Tantras of Unexcelled Highest Yoga Tantra, rooted in the Guhyasamaja and Heruka Chakrasamvara tantras.

Your Support Matters

We invite you to become an integral part of the Badawa Academy's mission. Your support can take many forms:
1. Share the Wisdom: Share the teachings and insights you gain from our book and the Badawa Academy's curriculum with your friends, family, and colleagues. Extend the gift of Nirvana Wisdom to those around you.
2. Financial Support: Consider making a donation to the academy. Your contribution will help sustain our mission and enable us to reach more individuals in need of profound transformation. We are currently

working on translating four classical Buddhist texts specially chosen by Garab Tulku into English. We have completed the translation of almost half of the Collection of Topics Text titled 'A Jewel Lamp to Illuminate the Characteristics of Phenomena', which is expected to span approximately 500 pages. This text book will serve as the foundational course for Badawa Academy.
3. Volunteer: If you have time, skills, or resources to share, consider volunteering at the academy. Your involvement can make a tangible impact on the lives of our students and the success of our programs.
4. Continue Your Journey: Deepen your own spiritual practice by enrolling in courses at Badawa Academy, attending retreats, and participating in workshops. Your personal growth is a testament to the academy's teachings.

Your support, in whatever form it takes, is instrumental in ensuring that the wisdom of the Badawa Academy continues to shine brightly, offering solace and enlightenment to all seekers. Together, we can usher in a world where meaningfulness, peace, and wisdom prevail.

Thank you for being a part of our community and for considering how you can contribute to the growth and success of the Badawa Buddhist Academy. May Nirvana Wisdom guide your path towards a life filled with purpose and serenity.

With heartfelt gratitude,

Garab Tulku Lobsang Dhonden

Visit us at www.badawa-academy.org
tibetanbookofhappiness@gmail.com

ABOUT THE AUTHOR

Garab Tulku Lobsang Dhonden was born in 1976 in the Bimangtang family of the last Regent of Tibet, His Holiness Tadrak Dorjechang. In search of Buddha's heart teaching, under the kind guidance of His Holiness the Dalai Lama, he became a monk and joined Gaden Shartse Monastery in 1991. He proceeded through the 15 year program of Buddhist philosophical studies and completed it with flying colors in 2005. On the 27th of January, 2007 he was conferred the title of Geshe, the Tibetan equivalent of a Ph.D. in Buddhism.

Teachers

His main teachers are His Holiness the Dalai Lama, Abbot Emeritus His Eminence Lati Rinpoche, Abbot Emeritus His Eminence Jampa Yeshi, and two renowned 20th century yogis who spent their entire lifetimes in meditation in the forest, Gen Lamrimpa and Gen Nyima.

Tulku Recognition

On February 20, 1992 His Holiness the Dalai Lama recognized Rinpoche as the reincarnation of the 5th Garab Lobsang Tsultrim Tenpai Nyima who was the abbot of Sonak monastery in the Amdo Rebkong region of Tibet.

Rinpoche has conducted teachings, lectures, and healing sessions world-wide, including the United States, Spain, Germany, Italy, France, Greece, Singapore, and Malaysia. His teachings on the Buddhist way of happiness have been well received; even non-Buddhists throng to his lectures and classes. Rinpoche is currently working on establishing 'Badawa Buddhist Academy', which offers comprehensive Buddhist studies designed to cultivate Nirvana Wisdom.

Printed in Great Britain
by Amazon